The Literature of Cinema

ADVISORY EDITOR: **MARTIN S. DWORKIN**
INSTITUTE OF PHILOSOPHY AND POLITICS OF EDUCATION
TEACHER'S COLLEGE, COLUMBIA UNIVERSITY

THE LITERATURE OF CINEMA presents a comprehensive selection from the multitude of writings about cinema, rediscovering materials on its origins, history, theoretical principles and techniques, aesthetics, economics, and effects on societies and individuals. Included are works of inherent, lasting merit and others of primarily historical significance. These provide essential resources for serious study and critical enjoyment of the "magic shadows" that became one of the decisive cultural forces of modern times.

Musical Accompaniment of Moving Pictures

Edith Lang and George West

ARNO PRESS & THE NEW YORK TIMES

New York • 1970

Reprint Edition 1970 by Arno Press Inc.
Reprinted by permission of The Boston Music Company
Reprinted from a copy in The Museum of Modern Art Library
Library of Congress Catalog Card Number: 72-124014
ISBN 0-405-01620-4
ISBN for complete set: 0-405-01600-X
Manufactured in the United States of America

MUSICAL ACCOMPANIMENT
OF MOVING PICTURES

A Practical Manual
for

PIANISTS AND ORGANISTS

AND AN EXPOSITION OF THE PRIN-
CIPLES UNDERLYING THE MUSICAL
INTERPRETATION OF MOVING PICTURES

By

EDITH LANG

AND

GEORGE WEST

Price, $1.25 net

The Boston Music Company.
Boston. Mass.

G. SCHIRMER · New York   WINTHROP ROGERS, LTD. · London

Printed in the U. S. A.

CONTENTS

INTRODUCTION

THAT *music* is an invaluable and necessary aid to the success and enjoyment of moving pictures, is a fact which no one will deny. But the accompanying, or illustrating, music must be of the *right kind*, or else its very aim will be defeated. Unfortunately, the right kind of "picture music" is something that is not universally understood, and the musician, no matter how learned he may be in his trade, is beset by a great many problems, when he attempts to follow and illustrate in music the fast-moving film. This book is not intended to exhaust a subject which is almost unlimited in its aspects, but it rather endeavors to lay down a few safe and dependable rules and courses of action from which any student of these problems may make his own deductions and develop his own personal style. For nothing would be more tedious or impracticable than to attempt uniformity where variety and individuality are the essentials. The most successful and highest-paid player is the one whose style is the most distinctive. When you analyze this distinction, you will find that it is mainly based on certain characteristics of his personality, such as intelligence, quick perception, realization of dramatic values, insight in human psychology, and well-grounded musical technique. But aside from these factors, there is one quality which the player requires above all, and which this book primarily intends to awaken and develop. That quality is resourcefulness.

With resourcefulness the average player of even mean endowments may fit himself to follow any kind of picture that may be thrown on the screen. This resourcefulness extends in two different directions: one of them is the musical training which must aim to perfect facility in improvisation; the other is a cultivation of taste and a sense of fitness in adapting musical material to the pictured scene. We shall try, in the following paragraphs, to give practical hints in both of these directions. Therefore this book may be considered as a "first-aid" manual for the beginner in the field of moving picture music.

The prime function of the music that accompanies moving pictures is to reflect the mood of the scene in the hearer's mind, and rouse more

1

readily and more intensely in the spectator the changing emotions of the pictured story.   One hears much music in the "movies" that is as foreign to the action on the screen as anything could be, and frequently actually kills the effect of the photographer's art.   Producers have been quick to realize this danger, and therefore many pictures are being released with minute instructions concerning the music that is to accompany them. (See ill. p. 60.)   But even so, the player will require some training to do the music and the picture justice, and will succeed best if his mental alertness and his musical resourcefulness work hand in hand.

PART I

EQUIPMENT

1. Mental Alertness

The player will do well, first of all, to "size up" his audience. Hardly two theatres in any place cater to exactly the same crowd. What "goes" in one house, "falls flat" in another. He will therefore have to experiment and judge carefully what road to follow. But it should be stated right at the beginning, and strongly emphasized, that most audiences are misjudged in that they are capable of much more education and cultivation than they are generally given credit for. He is a lazy and sterile player who is satisfied that what he is giving his audience is "good enough." The standards of good and bad music may vary according to country and clime. But it would not be hard to agree on desirable and undesirable material for the musical accompaniment of moving pictures. Its first requisite is fitness. The player will determine this according to his lights and to the measure of his taste. It is well to choose from among the contemporaneous popular music such numbers as have become identified with certain emotions, either of patriotism, joy, or sadness. The audience will grasp quickest what it is fairly familiar with, and sometimes a short strain from, or mere suggestion of, a popular number will go a long way toward telling its story. The classical repertoire, on the other hand, is an inexhaustible treasure trove for all who seek diligently and patiently.

As the musical interpreter of the emotions depicted on the screen, the player himself must be *emotional* and respond to the often quick changes in the situation. In fact, if not his knowledge of life, his knowledge of the picture must enable him to *anticipate*, so that his music is always slightly ahead of the film, preparing rather than reflecting. Therefore *the player's eyes should be on the screen as constantly as possible*, and never for too long a stretch on the music or on the keyboard. His attention should be riveted on the turn of events, his emotions should promptly respond to pathos or humor, to tragedy or comedy, as they may be interwoven in the picture play. A keen sense of humor is a necessary requirement in his make-up. But his wit should be capable of attuning itself to various gradations, from subtle irony to broad "slap-stick" farce and horse-play.

3

Mental alertness is needed in quickly "locating" the *musical atmosphere* for a picture. If a scene is laid in, or suddenly shifted to the Orient, if in the news section of the performance the film should portray a scene in a foreign country, music of a corresponding nature will make the picture "get over" much more successfully than would the indifferent playing of a waltz tune. The player must be exceedingly careful not to "italicise" the situation so that it becomes distorted or burlesqued. Therefore he should refrain from all excesses. A case in point may be cited here. In the series of Burton Holmes's "travel pictures" the "Tagalog Toilers of Luzon" in the Philippines are shown, planters and reapers of rice. These toilers, hard-working men and women, are pictured in the act of threshing the cereal, which they accomplish by a peculiar and complicated treading of the sheaves with their feet, resembling for all the world a weird dance. With a monotonous rhythm in the bass and an exotic inflection of the melody, the strangeness and primitiveness of the scene would stand out, the long and patient toil of the threshers would be apparent, the photographer's aim would be gained. Instead, the musician plays a Broadway cabaret tune, with plenty of "jazz"; the house is roaring with laughter and the photographer's intended lesson is lost!

This leads to the remark that flippancy and facetiousness are wholly out of place in a serious and educational picture. The player's attitude of mind should always be one of interest, never betray tiredness or boredom. Nothing is more quickly sensed by an audience than the inattentiveness and indifference of the player.

In order to illustrate properly in music the happenings on the screen, the musician should be endowed with *psychological insight*. Many books on the subject are within reach of the student, and enough of them are written in so popular a vein that they can be understood and read with profit by the layman. Human nature, in spite of its complication, can be reduced to a rather limited field of observation, so far as the "movies" are concerned. There is more or less resemblance between a great many films. The intrigue is very often the same, the emotions follow each other in a given circle, the development varies but slightly. The law of compensation rules supreme, virtue receives its reward, crime its punishment. Love and hatred, hope and despair, harrowing moments of tension and episodes of comic relief make up the bulk of moving pictures. Such fundamental emotions, and their related affections, should be carefully studied by the player; he should be able readily to recognize them, and he should seek to express them in turn by means of music. In order to do this successfully, he should not wait until he is in the theatre and the film has started. He should devote hours of study to the carrying out of a preconceived plan by which he sets himself the task of playing or improvising music that corresponds to these basic moods of human nature. In other words, he should put himself successively into a frame of mind that is the equivalent of happiness or grief, of quiet contemplation or hurried flight, of hope attained or shattered dreams. With sympathetic curiosity he should study the mental processes by which human actions are guided, he should learn to distinguish between noble and dastardly motives. Music is a speech more subtle and pliant than that of mere words, and a sensitive player is capable of conveying, more clearly than the spoken word could do, what the thought or gesture of the film actor may imply.

The player should, above all, learn to *read facial expressions*. Since the actor, deprived of speech, must emphasize his emotions by facial play, the twinkle in his eye, a furrow of his brow, a look, or a smile are the only manifestations of his thought. These the player must learn to distinguish and to recognize instantly. Music, it may as well be stated, cannot always shift as quickly as will the facial play of the actor in some scene or other. It will then behoove the player to give the keynote of the situation with illustrative strains. However, a word of caution may be added here, that one should not rely too much on such methods, since nothing heightens the enjoyment and effect of a film more strongly than a close and minute following of every phase of the photo play, with due regard to musical continuity.

A *good memory* is a valuable help to the player. Not only should he try to memorize certain compositions as a whole, but he should especially furnish his storehouse of remembered music with stock phrases and motives, adapted to different moods, so that he can always draw from this library in his head. He should also try to remember certain films, the development of the story, the sequence of situations, so that he may anticipate the effect by recognizing the cause. Since popular wisdom has it that sunshine always follows upon rain, that the harvest shall be as the planting, the psychologist of the "movies" generally finds that the story of the film follows this popular line of thought. The memorizing of certain music that fits certain situations, of special musical effects that characterize particular incidents, is the surest way by which the player can keep himself always *ready for emergencies*. Thus alone can he gain security and ease in his playing!

It remains to say a few words about *"theatrical values."* The player should never forget that he is not playing an organ or piano recital, but that he is furnishing theatrical music for a theatrical production. Tragedy and comedy are built on the basis of ancient and well-recognized rules. As the play progresses, gains impetus, presents its problems and intrigues, gradually reaches its climax and leads to the solution, so should the music advance and follow the march of events with an ever increasing intensity.

The graphic illustration of certain theatrical situations will be treated of later. Suffice it here to say that there are times when a situation becomes so intense that even music fails to express it, and that nothing but a *moment of silence* can give an actual realization to the spectator. If a play demands "local color" the music should unmistakably give it or approximate it at least. The lighting of a picture, whether in full sunlight or veiled by the shadows of dusk, will govern the *intensity of tone* that the player draws from the instrument. The "speed" with which the action progresses will influence the *tempo of the music*. One may go so far as to say that the very scenery of the picture can be hinted at in tones. A peaceful, blossoming landscape will demand music different from that which will fit a bleak and desolate mountain region. The bustle of city life will require music of faster tempo than the placid village square.

Nothing can give a better idea of what good moving picture music should be, than the careful study of successful operas. Therein the welding of action and music is so close, that they cannot be separated; the musical characterization amounts to a labelling of each singer with a pertinent phrase or motive. Take as an instance the opera "Carmen" by Bizet. "Local color" is given by a predominance of rhythms familiarly associated with Spanish music. Watch the handling of the crowds, the excited populace in the first act, the hilarious dancers in the second, the mysterious smugglers in the third, the stately and gay procession in the fourth. Mark the voluptuous and alluring airs of Carmen herself, in the first act, contrasted with the simple and sweet melodies that are given to Micaela, the innocent country maiden. Note the dramatic effect of the motive of foreboding and doom, first sounded in the third act, when the cards invariably point to Carmen's death. The use of this motive, in the fourth act, becomes uncanny and achieves the height of theatrical impressiveness. One of the finest modern examples of graphic stage music is Puccini's opera "Tosca." Each character is treated in a manner that reveals the essential traits of his or her nature. Every measure in the orchestra fits the situation on the stage. Love scenes of unequalled fervor are followed by those of brutality, of tragedy and horror. Attention should be called to the beautiful portrayal in music of dawn breaking over the city of Rome, at the beginning of the third act.

Similar instances could be named without number. The diligent student will search for himself in the vast operatic literature for passages that become universally adaptable and will form his most effective stock in trade. Then, there are a great many songs which by their words have become associated with certain thoughts or emotions, and which the player should be able to call upon without the notes, if necessary. There are a great many pleasing salon pieces of the lighter kind that will prove particularly useful for comedies and some of the shorter film plays.   Music generally associated with such events as weddings, funerals, patriotic exercises, parades, special seasons of the year, boat songs, college songs, church hymns, and the like, should all be in the player's fingers, ready to answer instantaneous calls.

2. Musical Resourcefulness

a. *General Remarks*

It goes without saying that the player should constantly aim to improve his musicianship and to develop his technique, that of the fingers alone, if he uses the piano, that of keys and pedals, if he plays the organ.   Since the latter instrument has become predominant in most moving picture houses, we shall concentrate upon its special technique.   This calls immediately for a word regarding organ registration.   The player should familiarize himself with the peculiarities of each stop, select the most effective, and avoid the defective or blatant ones.   As a guide for his *registration*, the player should always have the *orchestra* in mind!   As varied in tone color as this body of instruments is, so should be the change and relief obtained by a wise and frequent variation in stops.

Registers and tone qualities of the organ should be kept separate and clear, such as strings alone, flute alone, reeds (oboe, saxophone, French horn, cornopean, etc.), alone, whenever possible.   Tone qualities should no more be mixed promiscuously than all ten fingers should be put on the keys in long stretches of injudicious chord playing.   It is best to avoid close harmony.   It is generally safe to adhere to the effect of a *solo instrument with accompaniment*.   "Full organ" should be avoided except in special instances.   As a rule, the organ should rather suggest its presence than make itself overpoweringly felt.   The music must vitalize the action on the screen, not absorb the attention of the spectator, or deaden his ears.   In the "movies", a mere finger-acrobat becomes a nuisance.   On the other hand, it is dangerous to overwork soft stops and echo effects.   A constant "murmur" of the organ is most irritating.   Light and shade should vary according to the picture's progress.   If possible, one should not make a *crescendo* to full organ more than once during a picture.   An overuse of glaring and striking tone colors is undesirable.   To be sure, there are certain situations where nothing but a distinctive kind of reed will express either the diabolical expression of a face or the gruesomeness of a scene.   But "atmosphere" is more effective than strident noise.

The player should try to develop his musical resourcefulness chiefly by cultivating his talent for *improvisation*.   This does not necessarily mean that he must be gifted as a composer and originator of musical ideas, although this ability will prove his supreme asset.   But it will suffice if he learns to handle a given theme, or rather several of them, by the means of rhythmical or modal variation, by extension or diminution, by change of tone register and by contrapuntal combination.

b. *Musical Characterization*

The kernel of the musical illustration of a picture is the *main theme*. This should be typical in mood or character of the hero or heroine.   It should have emotional appeal, it should be easily recognizable and admit of such treatment as mentioned above.   This theme should be announced in the introduction, it should be emphasized at the first appearance of the person with whom it is linked, and it should receive its ultimate glorification, by means of tonal volume, etc., in the finale of the film.   Added to this, there will be as many subsidiary themes as there are secondary characters in the film.   This does not mean that every face that appears on the screen must be labelled with a musical motive.   This procedure applies only to the characters that are really concerned in the progress of the action.   The villain will be characterized by a sinister or sombre theme, the comedian by a light and frivolous one, and so on.

c. *Thematic Development*

The treatment and development of these musical themes, for purposes of picture accompaniment, is very much in the nature of the treatment given to a musical idea in the course of a composition such as a sonata or symphony.   But, while the player cannot be urged too strongly to study such works, the aim of this book will probably be best served by freeing the subject of its more intricate technicalities and by plainly stating a few methods through which this musical alteration or variation of a theme may be accomplished.

Let us take for instance an emotional theme such as :

Ex. A

Andante

Str 8, Fl 8'- Saxophone Solo - light string and flute accompaniment

If this theme were to represent the heroine in ordinary circumstances, her appearance under emotional stress or afflicted with sorrow might be characterized by playing the theme in the minor mode, as follows :

Ex. B

At a moment of hesitation, of doubt, or when placed in the necessity of making a decision, the heroine might be characterized by a "breaking" of the theme in the following manner:

Ex. C

Her anxiety might be expressed by taking the theme in a rhythmically quicker form, and if this anxiety was caused by pleasant anticipation, the theme would naturally be given in major:

Ex. D

while it would be given in minor, if her anxiety was caused by apprehension or fear, as follows:

Ex. E

Attention should be called to the way in which these various examples are treated with respect to registration and accompaniment. They will offer an outlook on the great variety that may be accomplished by judicious manipulation.   Only a few basic emotions have here been illustrated.   A wider range of psychological insight will suggest to the player a greater number of possibilities in such manipulation.   The player should always seek to differentiate in each return of the theme, during the film, so that new interest will enhance its appeal.   An effective means of variation is offered by placing the melody in a lower register and ornating it in the treble with appropriate figure work, as given here:

Ex. F

This treatment might suggest itself if the hero were pictured in a meditation of which the heroine is the subject, or if he were reading a letter received from her, in other words, if the heroine did not actually enter into the picture but if the thought of her was implied by the action of others.   The "mood" of a theme can be totally changed by altering the rhythm.   For instance, our theme, originally played in common time, gains in "lightness" and airiness if presented in three-four time.

Ex. G

Such treatment will be appropriate for a scene in which the heroine is pictured in particularly pleasant and happy circumstances or actually dancing. On the other hand, a theme that was originally presented in three-four time:

Ex. H

might be given "weight" by lengthening the measure into one of four-four, as follows:

Ex. I

Greater emotional intensity will be suggested by playing the original theme to an accompaniment of nine-eight.

Ex. J

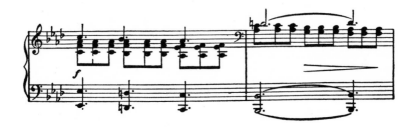

All such variations should be accompanied by change in organ registration.   While it is not easy to identify each stop or tone color with a special character or emotion, it may be 'safe to recommend, for purposes of general guidance, the indications given on pages 54 and 55.

What has been said with regard to the theme characterizing the heroine, applies equally to any other that may be chosen for the hero.   But in all cases, these themes should be sufficiently *"striking,"* so that the audience can easily identify and remember them.   In all their changes they should remain easily recognizable.   Therefore it might be said that ordinarily a theme that moves diatonically, that is step-wise, will not stand out so well as one that has at least one or two skips.   For example:

is preferable to

As we said before, not only persons may be characterized by musical themes, but also localities.   If, for instance, the action is laid recurrently in a certain place, this *locality* should always be announced by the same theme.   However, variation is essential here, as in other cases; and if we may take for example a garden scene, this garden in sunlight might be characterized as follows:

while the same place, shrouded in twilight, might suggest the following treatment of the theme:

As a matter of course, different weather conditions will demand different music. On page 57 you will find suggestions for rain, for the approach and breaking of a thunderstorm, etc. However, all those effects are individually distinctive and are not the result of thematic "development."

Hand in hand with changes of thematic variation, of organ registration, and of time, should go judicious changes in *tonality*. The player should be cautioned that, when selecting his themes, he see to it that they are *not all in the same key*, so that he achieve in the course of his performance a pleasing variety of tonalities. Nor is it advisable to adhere for too long a time to tonalities that are all in flats, or to those that are all in sharps. Sometimes a player has certain likes and dislikes for given keys. These he should eliminate and make himself proficient in all of the keys. It is particularly objectionable when the player slavishly adheres to the "black keys," and gives a whole evening's performance in D-flat or G-flat. There are certain keys such as A-flat and E-flat which suggest "warmth" or languor, such as B-flat minor or G minor which fit a mood of sorrow and grief, such as A or D major which lend themselves to brilliancy, such as E major which suggests "clear skies" or "the ocean's wide expanse." Said ocean, lashed into rollers by the fury of the wind, will naturally demand more agitated music than the placid surface in a calm, and possibly the player may find that he will also wish to differentiate in a key in which this raging element may find a fit illustration. Melodies of a meditative character or of a religious nature often gain when played in the key of F. The key of C has nothing to commend it, except that after long wanderings through the rich realms of sharp or flat tonalities, it is most gratifying to hear the crisp and bright "key of keys." These suggestions, in regard to the nature and individual color of certain keys, are approximations, at best, and experiments have shown that different people react differently to the effect of various keys. But at least they will make the player curious to investigate for himself and serve to make him realize that there exists a distinction between one tonality and another. He will quickly see that "transposition" from one key to another will lend to his theme a varied aspect and that it forms one of the *easiest ways* of *obtaining contrast*.

d. *Transition and Modulation*

This leads to one of the most important points to which the player should give special attention and continued study, namely to that of smooth musical *transition* or effective *modulation*. By the scope given to this subject in the textbooks on harmony, it can be easily seen how essential its mastery is. The player who is not already familiar with this chapter of musical harmony will do well to enlarge his knowledge by carefully reading chapter XI in J. Humphrey Anger's "Treatise on Harmony," part I.

For the practical use of the "movie" player there are, however, certain "tricks" of modulation which it may be well to point out here. As a general rule the player should bear in mind that his transitions should never be abrupt, unless a special graphic end may be gained thereby. He should take time and care with his modulations. But what the following examples intend to teach, is more a principle than an application. Only continued practice will make the application a matter of ease and surety.

The simplest modulations are the natural ones from one key into its related keys, namely those of the (1) dominant, (2) sub-dominant, (3) relative, and (4) parallel minor keys; or for instance: from C major to (1) G (major), (2) F (major or minor), (3) A minor, and (4) C minor. There is hardly a composition in which one or several of these modulations are not used; they may be readily found in any text-book. However, text-book demonstrations are generally, and for the sake of clearness, written in chord progressions which form the harmonic skeleton of the melodic progress. Such presentation as the following:

may admirably show the underlying harmonies, which, properly connected, form the basis of a modulation from one key to its two chromatically adjacent keys (from C to Cb, or from C to C#), but they will decidedly *not* do for our purposes. The player should, in fact, carefully shun anything that sounds like the wearisome chord progressions favored by diligent and patient piano tuners. The text-book style of 4-part harmony, at its best, too closely resembles church music; and unless a picture actually shows a church or religious function, the suggestion of the organ as an instrument associated with religious worship should be strictly avoided in the theatre. The many voices of the organ should always approximate the quality of an orchestra, and only in particular cases remind you of the choir loft! Nevertheless, the study of textbooks on harmony, and principally on modulation, is an invaluable help in understanding, and carrying on independently, the exposition that follows.

Even the quickest and most abrupt modulation that the turn of events, as pictured on the screen, may necessitate, should be made to act as a *melodic* (or thematically connecting) link as well as a harmonic bridge. No matter how short a motive may be, it will always serve to emphasize the organic nature of a modulation. It may either echo a theme that is about to be discarded, or anticipate a new one that is to be introduced.

Which method the player should follow depends somewhat on the picture, namely whether the action is receding from a moment of intensity (in which case the "intense" motive will be "reëchoed") or whether it is progressing to such a moment (in which case the "intense" motive will act as a "foreboding"). These simple devices offer specimens of the many "psychologic" possibilities of modulation in connection with the proper use of motives and special themes.

In modulating from one key ("given key") to another ("prospective key"), it may be found that the related keys (see above) of the prospective key are more easily reached than the prospective key itself. In such cases the modulation will, of necessity, be a little more circuitous; but what it loses in directness, it will gain in musical effectiveness. It makes the modulation more "convincing," if the prospective key is reached by way of its relative minor key, or by way of its sub-dominant. The most obvious method, and that which in all cases may be regarded as the safest approach, is a *modulation to the dominant of the prospective key.* With the seventh degree added to the tonic triad of the dominant key, the dominant-seventh chord of the prospective key is established, and from it the modulation will drop logically into the tonic triad of the prospective key. For example, G being the dominant of C, the chord becomes and leads into . Therefore the player will do well to practice such modulations at the keyboard, aiming to reach the (1) dominant, or (2) subdominant, or (3) relative minor, or (4) parallel minor keys of the prospective key. But such procedure, while of excellent musical effect, is often lengthy and might prevent the player from following the speed of pictured events. Hence, for purposes of instantaneous or quick modulation, the following methods are recommended.

I. Modulation with the ⎰ unaltered (see Ex. Ia–IVa and Ib–IVb)
   aid of *pivotal note* ⎱ enharmonically changed (see Ex. V and VI).

II. Modulation with the ⎰ unchanged (see Ex. VIIa, b, c)
   aid of *pivotal chord* ⎱ chromatically altered (see Ex. VIIIa, b, c).

III. Modulation with the ⎰ in the "given key" so as to suggest, or
   aid of *motive altered* ⎱ lead into the "prospective key" (see Ex. IX).

IV. Modulation with the aid of *diminished-seventh chords* (see Ex. X).

I. With regard to the first method, it becomes at once apparent that the success of its employment depends largely upon the selection of the proper tone as pivot. In the examples Ia–IVa, and Ib–IVb, the same modulations have been effected by the use of different pivotal notes, all of which serve the purpose. By analyzing the examples the player will find that the notes of the "given" chords which were *not* used as pivots would have probably proved less helpful to, if not actually prevented, a smooth and convincing progression.

Pivotal note (*) unaltered:

Ex. Ia

NB.   If a B♭ is substituted for the B♮, the modulation "tends" towards G minor, and from there E♭ major, A♭ major or minor, etc. may be reached.

Ex. IIa

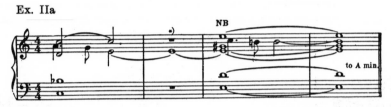

NB.   With a C♯ instead of the C♮, the modulation will "tend" towards A major, and from there to F♯ minor, etc.

Ex. IIIa

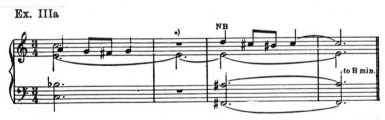

NB.   With good effect, a D♯ could replace the D♮, and the modulation would then lead to B major, or from there to G♯ minor and major, or F♯ major, etc.

Ex. IVa

NB.   With a G♮ and C♮ in the chord, instead of the G♯ and C♯, the modulation leads to E minor, and from there to C major, or any other related and accessible key.

Ex. Ib

Ex. IIb

Ex. IIIb

Ex. IVb

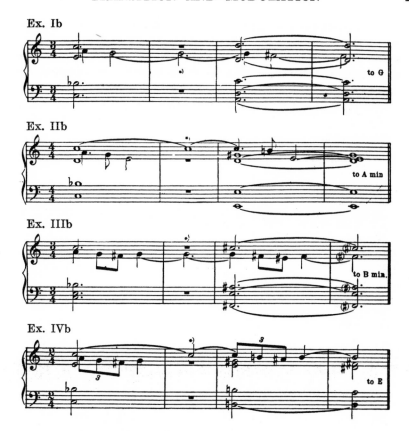

Pivotal note (*) enharmonically changed.

Ex. V

Compare this modulation with Ex. III!

Ex. VI

In this example *two* notes form the pivotal link, one of which is enharmonically changed, the other remains unaltered.

II. The success of the second method is dependent on a quick discernment as to which of the notes in the "given" chord will point by either *suspension* [1] or *anticipation* [2] to the "prospective" chord.. The devices of suspension and anticipation are most valuable aids in modulation, and, if tastefully employed, will greatly enhance the music.   And yet it may not be out of place to say here a word against the abuse of "chromatically" creeping modulations, which soon become cloying and lose the inherent charm which they possess when used with moderation.

Pivotal chord, unchanged:

Ex. VII

Pivotal chord, chromatically altered:

Ex. VIII

---

[1] A *suspension* is the name given to a discord formed by the *holding over*, or prolongation, of a note from one chord to which it belongs into another to which it does not belong; this dissonant note is then resolved by rising or falling (usually the latter) *one degree* to the note to which it would have proceeded directly had it not been held over.   It is possible to hold over more than one note from one chord to another, viz. two or three, etc., when the suspension is called double or triple, etc.

[2] An *anticipation* is the name given to a dissonant note introduced into one chord and held over, as a consonant note, in the succeeding chord.   Sometimes double and triple anticipations are employed.

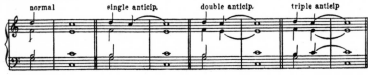

III. For practical purposes, the third of these methods is undoubtedly one of the simplest and quickest. It is advisable to lead into the "transitory recitative" (first measures of Ex. IX) without "straining" or altering the tonality, so that the "given" key is established before the transition begins. But in cases of emergency, for which this method is invaluable, the "transitory recitative" may be taken up almost at *any* point, so long as the outline of the *motive*, no matter how much it may be chromatically or diatonically altered, remains sufficiently recognizable. The "transitory recitative" is virtually the melody in a chain of modulating chords, in which these chords have been omitted. If they are replaced, as in IXf (which achieves the same modulation as IXe, where they are omitted) it cannot be truthfully said that this replacement, heavy and "text-bookish" as it sounds, adds anything to the modulation, in beauty or effectiveness. On the contrary, it sounds involved and sluggish.

Modulatory recitative:

Ex. IX

IV. Any diminished-seventh chord, such as that given in Ex. X, in all of its inversions, is a means of instantaneous modulation. In Ex. X the same diminished-seventh chord, in its various inversions, is made to serve as a modulatory link to the dominant-seventh chord of all the twelve tonalities (major and minor) which are comprised in our present musical system. That the dominant-seventh chord, in all twelve cases, is introduced by the suspension of one of the notes in the chord, is not a matter of accident; it cannot be stated too often that by the aid of suspensions smoothness will be added to almost every modulation.

Modulation with a diminished-seventh chord:

Ex. X

The introduction of the diminished-seventh chord itself is a matter demanding but little skill. For any one, though only just beginning to be familiar with the art of improvisation, will quickly see how easily a melodic phrase may be deflected into a chord of this nature. Ex. XI will demonstrate this with the aid of our original theme.

Ex. XI

As a matter of fact, both Ex. XIa and XIb lead each into a different diminished-seventh chord, the one reached at the conclusion of XIb being identical with the one from which Ex. X proceeds. The player will notice that a very pleasing effect may be obtained by joining Ex. XIa and b, and he will pay particular attention to the fact that from the close of Ex. XIb he may *immediately* go into the *second* measure of *any one* of the twelve examples in Ex. X. This, and similar experiments, should be repeatedly and diligently tried, for they are invaluable in giving the player that musical resourcefulness of which the ability quickly and effectively to modulate forms such an important part. It cannot be too highly recommended to all students, seriously desiring to perfect themselves in this field, that they combine with the absorption of the hints, given above, a careful study of modulatory devices as presented in text-books and, most of all, in the works of the masters. The piano compositions of Chopin, Schumann, Liszt, and César Franck will prove an inexhaustible source of instruction and inspiration. Only by going to works of art for the necessary model, may the player eventually hope to shape his task into another expression of musical art, and so gain the true purpose of his mission. In the selection of modulatory devices, as in everything else, the player should carefully refrain from adhering too closely or exclusively to one and the same form. Mannerisms and bad habits are easily acquired. Variety is the principal aim that should be sought.

e. *Transposition*

Another valuable source of help to the player is his ability to *transpose* any piece of music, theme or motive, into any key. Such faculty pre-supposes a certain familiarity with harmony and with the principal types of chords. To read at sight a composition in a key, different from that in which it appears on the printed page, demands training and mental alertness. .If the player should try to transpose each note into the higher or lower interval desired, as the piece progresses, he would find it slow work and impossible to give an adequate performance of the piece. In order to overcome this obstacle the player should learn to read melodies by giving them a universal scale-appellation, not according to the actual pitch of each note but to the degree which it represents in the scale of that particular piece. In other words, he should give each of the seven degrees of the scale its general scale-appellation,

$$do - re - mi - fa - sol - la - ti$$

so that the third degree of the scale, no matter in what key, will always be *mi,* or the sixth degree always *la.* Thus, if he has learned to read the

"Star-Spangled Banner" according to this method, he will read the beginning as

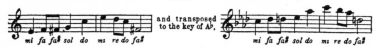

sol mi   do mi sol   do   mi re   do mi fa♯   sol

and be able to transpose the melody, with its proper harmonies, into any other key by simply adjusting the tonic *do* to the key desired. The melody of our theme would read accordingly, in the original Key of C,

and transposed to the key of A♭.

mi fa fa♯ sol do   mi re do fa♯   mi fa fa♯ sol do   mi re do fa♯

The symbol of ♯ before the 3d and 9th notes of the melody simply signifies that the notes are *raised* a semi-tone; as is seen in the transposition, the raise is actually effected by a ♮, since the degree of *fa* in the scale of A♭ has a "flat." This leads to the remark that in transposition from a key with sharps into a key with flats, the ♯ becomes a ♮, the x becomes a ♯, the ♮ becomes a ♭, the ♭ becomes a ♭♭; and on the other hand, in transposing from a key with flats into a key with sharps, the ♭ becomes a ♮, the ♭♭ becomes a ♭, the ♮ becomes a ♯, and the ♯ becomes a x. One of the simpler transpositions is that in which the notes on the staff remain the same, only the key signature is altered, as for instance from G to G♭, in which case the signature of one sharp turns into one of six flats. In transposing from the key of A♭ to that of A natural, the signature changes from four flats to three sharps, and all accidentals are altered in the way indicated above.

In order to verify and assimilate these rules, it will prove most helpful to carry out a few transpositions on paper, first a semitone up and down, with the notes remaining the same on the staff and only a change in accidentals taking place, later choosing larger intervals of transposition, at which to raise or lower the key, in which instances the notes on the staff also will change. However, *all intervals* of the original remain relatively *the same* in the transposed key, and by reading intervals instead of notes, that is, by adopting the substitution of general scale degrees (*do — re — mi* etc.) for the actual notes played, this transposition may be effected with ease and a measure of surety that depends only on the greater or lesser experience of the player.

f. *Improvisation*

The talent for musical improvisation is closely linked with that of musical composition. As a rule, great composers, and among them particularly those who excelled as organists — such as Bach, Mendelssohn, and Franck —possessed that gift to a supreme degree. Hence, the acquisition of a certain facility in improvising is equivalent to a study of the principles involved in composition, added to keyboard proficiency.

Since the study of composition presupposes familiarity with the rules of harmony, a book like "Keyboard Harmony," by Uselma C. Smith, does not only impart the necessary knowledge, but presents it at once in a manner which makes it applicable to the practical use of the student. The first thing to learn is the nature of the various scales, intervals and chords; next, the proper joining of chords; finally the arrangement of chords in musical cadences and phrases.

To improvise at the keyboard, means to let one's natural musical fancy dictate to the fingers, while one's acquired critical faculty constantly directs and supervises the result of that dictation. It may also be called "listening to an inner voice," which voice need not always be essentially original, but will often, and certainly at first, reëcho with a slightly different inflection outer voices that the player has heard before and now vaguely remembers.

In order to awaken a tendency for improvisation, you should try to SING a short melody of not more than eight measures, or eight accented beats, and see that the melody you sing does not actually resemble some other tune that you know. In doing this you will have made the first step on the road to improvisation. Be sure to REMEMBER the melody that you have thus created, by singing it over and by listening carefully to it until you have firmly settled it in your mind. Then ascertain the rhythm of your melody, and see whether it is in common time, in $\frac{3}{4}$ time or in some other rhythm. When you have done this, you should try to realize the position of the melody's first note in the scale (*i.e.* whether the melody begins with *mi, sol, do*, or any other degree of the scale), locate the pitch of the melody on the piano or organ to correspond to that in which you have been singing it, and then PLAY your melody on the keyboard. Let us take as an example an obvious melody, that might begin as follows:

You will see that the musical phrase (I) is built on a motive (1) which corresponds to a rhythm of two eighth notes followed by a quarter note. This rhythmical motive is repeated, or answered, by the identical rhythm but with different notes, for simple reasons of symmetry (one of the fundamental principles in musical composition), thus forming one half of the first phrase; the next half contains as many notes as the first, but they are rhythmically grouped in a different order. Phrase (II) follows the rhythmic scheme of (I). Let us assume the melody continues in the following way:

In the third phrase we encounter the rhythmic motive of the beginning reversed, *i.e.*, one quarter note followed by two eighth notes, then answered by its original form, the whole constituting one half of the phrase; the second half is rhythmically identical with the first half. In the fourth phrase, the first half is a rhythmic repetition of the melody's very beginning, and the conclusion of the phrase, being also the end of the melody, imitates rhythmically the conclusions of the first and second phrase, but comes to a stronger and more decided stop on the third beat of the measure (instead of on the fourth).

Thus we have analyzed the rhythmical skeleton of the melody. That it is composed of four groups of two measures each is not a matter of accident. As a rule, and the exceptions need not find consideration here, musical phrases are built up by linking groups of two measures into sentences of four measures, or any multiples thereof.

Let us now consider the melodic outline of our tune. The first three notes, forming our rhythmic motive, are ascending step by step; they are answered by a descending figure which starts one tone higher than the first motive ends, but descends to the same note with which the measure began. This first measure in turn is answered by a figure which follows the same melodic curve of ascent and descent, but is rhythmically varied. The third measure starts in imitating the first, but reaches higher in its second half, and is followed by a measure that brings the two phrases to a half-close. The fifth measure establishes a new melodic pattern by making a bold descent, stepwise, from the first to the last note of the measure; this pattern is repeated in the sixth measure. The seventh measure imitates the melodic curve of the very beginning, as does the eighth measure, only that this drops to the lowest tone of the whole melody and then settles in the final note.

The next step for the student is to try to hear the harmonic basis that underlies the melody. He may experiment at the keyboard with the chords that his harmonic knowledge place at his command, and he may achieve only the most primitive results such as shown in Ex. (1).

Ex. (1)

If his harmonic knowledge and his inner ear enable him to detect and hear a more varied harmonic treatment, he may play the melody as presented in Ex. (2) and (3).

Ex. (2)

Ex. (3)

It should be stated that the four-part harmonization of Ex. (2), while harmonically more interesting and aesthetically more pleasing than Ex. (1), is nevertheless too much after the "text-book" fashion, and therefore far removed from what the picture organist should strive for. The treatment of the accompaniment in Ex. (3) is more in the style of what the player should always hold before him as his goal, an expressive melody, unencumbered by middle voices, and simply seconded by chords that form a proper harmonic sequence, broken up, or figurated, in an appropriate manner. It would lead too far to present here all the problems that the player will meet with in improvising. But let it be clearly understood that this improvisation should not be a more or less dexterous finger play. The fingers should always be the interpreters of a song, or inner voice, that the player develops and carries in his mind. Only thereby can he hope to impart to his melodies their chief quality, which is *expressiveness*. He will naturally hear every tune in a certain harmonic garb, and to disclose this, as well as the tune itself, he must exercise his harmonic sense. For the carrying on, and thematic development, of a melody, a very excellent practical guide may be found in a little work on "Extemporization" by Dr. Frank J. Sawyer. The methods of improvisation will thereby become easily understood, and the student will be enabled to work the problems out for himself with a reasonable degree of surety. As a further practical help, no book could be recommended more strongly than Edmondstoune Duncan's "Melodies and How to Harmonize Them," which has the inestimable advantage of possessing a key by the same author, and published separately, which will supply the student with an answer to all the exercises, should he find difficulties in solving them.

With these remarks we bring to a close the general recommendations that every player for the pictures should bear in mind. *Mental alertness* and *musical resourcefulness* will enable any one who is gifted with sufficient technique to give a most adequate musical interpretation of the pictured scene. With a certain facility in improvisation and a sense of dramatic values, the player may even hope to accomplish more than that, and really give the spectator that most illusive of all experiences, a thrill!

3. REPERTOIRE

The following list, without attempting to be exhaustive, will furnish the player with enough suggestions to make his repertoire a large and varied one. It cannot be emphasized too strongly, that constant and diligent search for new material is all-important. With the study of the classification given herewith, the player will learn to distinguish musical moods and will gain surety in selecting the proper material for each scene that he may encounter.

NATURE

Bull	Melody	Friml	Iris
Carvel	Daffodils	Friml	Cherry Blossoms
Clough-Leighter	In the Woodland	Friml	Woodland Echoes
Grieg	Morning Mood	Lind	Evensong
Meyer-Helmund	In the Moonlight	Marshal-Loepke	Falling Snow
Nevin	Country Dance	Moter	In the Country
Nevin	Song of the Brook	Orth	By the Ocean
Nölck	Dancing Butterflies	Palmgren . . .	May-night
Saint-Saens . .	The Swan	Davis	Pastorale
Seeboeck . . .	The Hunt	Chaffin. . . .	In Springtime
Shackley . . .	Song of the Brook	Boisdeffre . . .	By the Brook
Whelpley . . .	Song of the Fountain	Coerne	Twittering Birds
Whelpley . . .	At Evening	Backer-Gröndahl	Summer Song
Helm	Sylvan Sketches	Bohm	Murmuring Brook

LOVE THEMES

Bernheimer . .	Romance	Whelpley . . .	Album-leaf
Cadman . . .	Melody	Sturgis	Meditation
Martel	Angelica	Hurst	Mélodie d'Amour
Elgar	Salut d'Amour	Grieg	I Love Thee
Gael	Voice of the Heart	Liszt	Love Dreams
Nevin	Love Song	Mitchell . . .	There was a Star
Svendsen . . .	Romance	Bohm	Cavatina
Quinn	Souvenir de Venise	Friml	Mélodie

LIGHT, GRACEFUL MOODS

Adam	Liselotte	Nesvera . . .	Butterflies
Berger	Capriccietto	Chaminade . .	Libellules
Seeboeck . . .	Le Dauphin	Delibes . . .	Pizzicati, "Sylvia"
Fomin	Lydia	Gillet	Babillage
Hellmesberger .	Entr'acte Valse	Grieg	Anitra's Dance
Huerter . . .	Caprice	Gabriel-Marie .	La Cinquantaine
Sanford . . .	Bluette	Moszkowski . .	Canzonetta

ELEGIAC MOODS

Bernheimer . .	Elegy	Huerter . . .	Yesterdays
Debussy . . .	Reverie	Huerter . . .	Told at Twilight
Mouton . . .	Enchanted Hour	Friml	Adieu
Nevin	Romance	Wagner . . .	Dreams
Palmgren . . .	The Swan	St. Quentin . .	Love's Meditation
Seeboeck . . .	Angelus	Raff	Cavatina
Szalit . . .	Intermezzo	Wolstenholm . .	The Answer
Wagner-Liszt . .	To the Evening Star	Rubinstein-Liszt	The Asra

IMPRESSIVE MOODS

Cui	Prelude in A♭	Wagner . . .	King's Prayer, from "Lohengrin"
Whelpley . . .	Prelude		
Hopekirk . . .	Sarabande	Wagner . . .	"Parsifal" Selections
Enesco	Adagio		
Halvorsen . . .	Triumphal Entry of the Boyars	Meyerbeer . .	Torch Dance
		Handel	Largo

FESTIVE MOODS

Nevin	Tournament	Verdi	March from "Aida"
Wagner . . .	March from "Tannhäuser"	Berlioz	Hungarian March
		Gounod . . .	Marche fanfare
Wagner . . .	Introduction to Third Act, "Lohengrin"	Gounod . . .	Marche pontificale
		de Koven . . .	Wedding March
Meyerbeer . .	Processional March, "The Prophet"	Chopin . . .	Polonaise militaire
		Ketterer . . .	Caprice militaire

EXOTIC MOODS

Oswald	Serenade Grise	Puccini . . .	Madama Butterfly
Adam	The Bim-Bims	Tschaikowsky .	Danse Arabe ("Nutcracker" Suite)
Albeniz . . .	Tango (Spanish)		
Albeniz . . .	Nochecita	Tschaikowsky .	Marche Slave
Manzanares . .	Oriental	Farwell . . .	American Indian Melodies
Luzatti . . .	Venetian Serenade		
Borch	From Russia	Gottschalk . .	Bamboula
Grunn	Zuñi Impressions	Loomis	Lyrics of the Redman
Peterkin . . .	Dreamer's Tales		
Saint-Saens . .	Ballet from "Samson and Delilah"	Luigini	Ballet Egyptien
		Rimsky-Korsakof	Chant Hindou

(See also page 42)

COMEDY

d'Ambrosio . .	En badinant (Chatterbox)	Huerter . . .	The Juggler Comedian
Clarke	A Day in Paris	Adam	Lancelot
Michel	Ninette	Bohm	Harlequin Polka
Monroe . . .	The Gobbler	Chadwick . . .	The Frogs
Wachs	Nadia	Lack	Pizzicato, Bluette
Huerter . . .	With Xylophone and Bells	Dumas	On the Hike
		Vollenhoven . .	The Rabbit

(See also page 37)

SPEED (Hurries)

Argus	Butterfly Chase	Alkan	The Wind
Barnby . . .	Will o' the Wisp	Bohm	Glissando Mazurka
Wachs	A travers l'espace	Gillet	The Humming Top
Musil	Frolic	Schubert-Heller .	Erlking
Chopin	"Minute" Waltz	Delibes	Passepied
Bach	Little Fugue, Gm.	Bossi	Scherzo, Gm.
Wagner . . .	Ride of the Valkyries	Noble	Morris Dance

NEUTRAL MUSIC

Chaminade . .	Air de Ballet	Godard . . .	Berceuse from
Densmore . . .	Gardenia		"Jocelyn"
Martel	Five Silhouettes	Godard . . .	Mazurkas (1–4)
Grieg	Lyric Pieces	Heller	Il penseroso
Mendelssohn . .	Songs without Words	MacDowell . .	Idyls
Liszt	Consolations	Moszkowski . .	Serenata
Henselt . . .	Spring Song	Schubert . . .	Moments musicaux
Henselt . . .	Were I a Bird	Wilm	Short Pieces, Op. 12
Friml	Chant sans Paroles	Tarenghi . . .	Serenata
Gillet	Sweet Caress	Karganoff . . .	Menuetto all'antico

WALTZES

Baynes	Destiny	Duval	Viennoise
Danglas . . .	On the Wings of Dream	Martel	Fleur-de-lis
		Delibes	Naïla

STANDARD OVERTURES

N. B. — Most of these overtures contain brilliant and lively passages which will fit scenes in the wild West, hurries, chases, fights, and mob scenes, etc.; many of them also contain slow movements which will prove useful as love themes, etc.

Rossini	William Tell	Herold	Zampa
Rossini	The Italians in Algeria (especially for detective stories)	Kela-Bela . . .	Hungarian Comedy
		Strauss	The Bat
		Mendelssohn . .	Midsummer Night's Dream
Nicolai	Merry Wives of Windsor (especially for fairy stories, etc.)	Hollins	Concert Overture, in C minor
		Weber	Oberon
		Weber	Freischütz
Suppé	Light Cavalry	Weber	Euryanthe
Suppé	Jolly Robbers	Mozart	Magic Flute
Suppé	Poet and Peasant	Mozart	Figaro's Wedding
Boieldieu . . .	Caliph of Bagdad	Beethoven . .	Egmont
Thomas . . .	Raymond	Beethoven . .	Coriolanus

SPECIAL CHARACTERS AND SITUATIONS

Tragedy

a. Impending:

Tschaikowsky	1st movement from Symphonie Pathétique
Beethoven .	1st movement from Sonata Pathétique
Rachmaninof	Prelude, C♯ minor

b. Aftermath:

Beethoven .	2d movement from Sonata Pathétique
Massenet . .	Elégie
Tschaikowsky	3d movement from Symphonie Pathétique

Death

Chopin . .	Funeral March
Beethoven .	Funeral March
Mendelssohn .	Funeral March

(N. B. — In the presence of actual death, observe silence!)

Battle Scenes

Tschaikowsky	Overture "1812"
Tschaikowsky	Last movement from Symphony No. 6

Storm Scenes

Rossini. . .	William Tell
Rachmaninof	Middle section from Prelude, C♯ minor
Beethoven .	1st movement from "Moonlight Sonata"

Villanous Characters

a. Robbers (In Drama)   Bizet . .   Smugglers' Chorus from "Carmen"
Robbers (In Comedy)   Grieg . .   In the Hall of the Mountain King
b. Sinister villain   Gounod . .   Music of Mephistopheles in "Faust"
c. Roué or vampire   Puccini . .   Music of Scarpia in "Tosca"
d. Revengeful villain   Leoncavallo   Introduction and finale from "Pagliacci"

Youthful Characters

Mendelssohn .	Spring Song
Grieg . . .	Spring Song
Grieg . . .	Butterflies
Nevin . . .	Mighty Lak a Rose

Old Age

Orth . . .	What the Old Oak Said
Danks . . .	Silver Threads Among the Gold
Hopekirk . .	Sundown

PART II

MUSICAL INTERPRETATION

1. THE FEATURE FILM

PERHAPS the best way of indicating a safe procedure in the musical interpretation of a feature film, is to single out one photo-play, and to suggest a musical garb that will fittingly clothe it with strains such as will bring out in bolder relief the plastic curves of the story. All of the motion picture concerns issue for each of the pictures which they release a synopsis that enumerates the various characters of the cast and gives an outline of the story. This synopsis should be carefully studied and should enable the player to select music descriptive of the various situations and emotions portrayed.

Let us take as an illustration "The Rose of the World" with Elsie Ferguson.[1] The opening scenes are laid in India, at a British Army Station. This will immediately suggest the necessity of preparing certain strains of music characteristic of the Orient; also of martial music in scenes depicting the soldier life. The story is as follows. Captain S. is married to a 16-year old girl named Rose, who is very beautiful, but as yet has not awakened to a realization of life and love. (1. *Main love theme, intensely emotional.*) The Captain is about to depart with his troops on a military expedition against rebellious natives. The film shows his leave-taking from the young wife; he tells her that if he returns alive he will teach her what love really means. The troops are seen departing in the distance, with the Captain in command, to the sound of Scottish bagpipes. (2. *Hindu motive interwoven with military march and imitation of bagpipes.*) The troops disappear, and Rose suddenly realizes her loss; she wildly longs for her husband. (3. *Main love theme repeated, with softer registration and rhythmically more agitated accompaniment.*) In the next scene, the return of the troops is shown. (4. *Same musical treatment as No. 2, going from faint to loud, and leading directly into 5. Introduction of Overture to the opera "William Tell."*) Rose looks in vain for her husband; the officers tactfully inform her that she is left a widow and hand

---

[1] By kind permission of The Famous Players-Lasky Corporation.

31

her a box of letters, the only thing that they are bringing back to remind her of her husband. (6. *Main love theme in the minor mode, suggestive of grief and despair.*) The next picture picks up events several years later, when Rose, believing herself a widow, has married the Viceroy of India, and a grand ball is held to celebrate the occasion. (7. *Brilliant waltz music.*) Lieut. R., a comrade of the late Captain S., appears and asks for permission to write the biography of his dead friend. (8. *"Somewhere a voice is calling."*) His request is granted. Rose's niece, a young school girl of "sentimental" age, falls in love with Lieut. R., and consequently is jealous of Rose, whose collaboration in the biography of her husband brings her much in contact with Lieut. R. The mischievous niece places a picture of the late Captain S. on the piano and begins to play and sing. (9. *Imitate school girl trying to play Grieg's "I love you."*) The niece's kitten helps in the performance by prowling leisurely over the keyboard. (10. *Imitate kitten skipping up and down the keys.*) Rose, exasperated, snatches the Captain's photo from the piano and rushes from the room. (11. *Agitated strain based on the main love motive.*) The biography has reached its closing chapter and Lieut. R. demands to see the box containing the late Captain's letters in order to make the story of the last moments complete. Rose feels that these letters are too sacred for the eyes of the outside world. (12. *Massenet's "Elégie," leading into an agitated strain*). Her husband, the Viceroy, without regard for the delicate feelings of Rose, demands that she surrender the letters in order to help Lieut. R. in his task. Rose realizes how repulsive her present husband is to her and how much she still loves her lost hero. (13. *Suggest the inner struggle of Rose by treating main love motive in minor mode and breaking it up in short phrases which successively rise in pitch, and finally lead into a calmer transition.*) The Viceroy has left Rose's boudoir; she gets out the box of letters and tries to read some of them; her emotion overcomes her and she faints. (14. *Nevin's "The Rosary"; endeavor to make the climax of the song synchronize with the moment at which Rose faints.*) Her health gradually fails and they decide to send her to England to recuperate. (15. *Suggestion of the Hindu theme leading into "Home, Sweet Home."*) Then follow scenes on the ocean liner and of the sea-voyage. (16. *"Sailor, beware."*) Rose returns to England, to the home of her first husband. (17. *"I hear you calling me."*) There she feels nearer to him in spirit, and spends much time in reading over his letters. (18. *Main love theme, with vibrato effects in the treble, and echo registration on the organ.*) She reads of the siege, the battle scenes, and his approaching death by thirst and starvation. (19. *Suggestion of Hindu music, agitated strains depicting the battle, leading into a tremendous climax.*) Suddenly the Viceroy and his Hindu secretary appear in the room. Her husband chides her, and becomes more loathsome in her eyes, the quarrel ending in a violent scene at the dinner table.

(20. *Snatches of the waltz, played for her wedding ball, suggested in a distorted and agitated manner, leading to a brutal outburst which accompanies the final confession of Rose, at the dinner table, that she loathes the Viceroy and belongs only to her first love.*) Rose rushes from the table and seeks to seclude herself in her own rooms. (21. *Suggest "Somewhere a voice is calling."*) In the night a terrible storm comes up. (22. *Storm music from Overture to "William Tell."*) Rose, in a frenzy, begs her Hindu maid to try an incantation that will bring back the spirit of Capt. S. (23. *Over a low rumbling in the bass, suggestive of the continued storm, the weird chant of the Hindu woman rises in the treble; this leads in a big crescendo to the climax.*) At the height of the storm and incantation, Capt. S. bursts into the room; he had escaped from the native prison, where he had been held a captive for three years, had managed to disguise himself as a Hindu and to find employment as the Viceroy's secretary. He had been watching to see if his wife still loved him. (24. *Main love theme.*) At the sight of the man whom she believed dead, Rose loses consciousness. Awakening the next morning, she finds her lover at her side; they are reunited, to live happily ever after. (25. *Apotheosis of main love theme.*)

Even this short exposition, briefly outlining the story, will show the variety of music required, and the manifold treatment which it needs, to depict graphically the emotions that animate each scene. Perhaps one of the most difficult things for the beginner to learn, is the joining together of musical motives and strains, as enumerated in the above example. It is here that musical taste and the ability to improvise will prove most valuable. Most of the emotions that come into play in the story just told are covered by the thematic variations demonstrated in an earlier chapter with the aid of our theme A. Thus, for instance, the music for number 6 would be treated similarly to our Ex. B. The music for No. 11 might be treated after the fashion of Ex. C. No. 13 might be dealt with according to Ex. E. For No. 18, Ex. F might serve as a model, by either using broken chords in the treble (as is the case in the example) or supplying the harmony by a vibrato in the treble. Ex. I might suggest the proper treatment for the return of the love theme at No. 24. For the apotheosis, or finale, at No. 25, Ex. A should be played with full organ, with rich and effective registration.

What has been said, under the general recommendations, regarding the necessity of varying constantly the time and key of the accompanying music, in order to avoid monotony, should naturally be borne in mind throughout the musical illustration of the feature film. The transition from one strain to another should be made with the aid of effective modulation, according to the principles laid down in an earlier paragraph. Variety of registration must add color to the music. The player should follow the story closely, and keep his eyes on the film as much as possible.

Experience will teach the player that for a great many occasions he will require what, for want of a better term, might be called "neutral" music. Thereby is meant music of no particular character, which forms a suitable accompaniment for scenes that do not call for special musical illustration. The type of music that will best serve this purpose is pleasant salon music, or some of the shorter preludes by Chopin, or some of the little piano pieces by Grieg. "Neutral" music should never last too long, as it is only a makeshift and a stop-gap.

2. "Flash-backs"

A peculiar feature of many films is the introduction of flash-backs. Thereby is meant the momentary interruption of the pictured story to give in a pictorial "flash" the thought of one of the actors, or to illustrate his words, or again to remind the audience of a secondary action which is supposed to go on at the same time in a different place.

Thus, for instance, a man, driven to despair, may be contemplating suicide. His emotional tension is illustrated in the music by gloomy or tragic accents. The man is about to shoot himself, when in his mind he suddenly sees the home of his childhood with his young orphan sister left to the mercies of this world, if he should destroy himself. The screen shows the old homestead, the sister in her sunbonnet picking flowers in the quaint and pretty garden. Nothing could be farther removed from the horror of the actual situation, than this picture of calm, of innocence and happiness. It fades as abruptly as it sprang up. But the thought of the consequences of his action have suddenly brought the man to realize the cowardice of his plan; he is determined to "stick it out" like a man. Now, it would be a mistake to interrupt the musical tension of the scene by introducing a few bars of "Garden music" while the girl is shown with her flowers; it would cut short the dramatic progress and foil the building up of a climax which comes when the man resolves to live, and throws away his gun. Therefore the music should not change its *character* during the flash-back, but it should be very much *subdued* and be instantly softened to a mere whisper while the flash-back is shown, to burst out immediately into normal loudness when the flash-back vanishes.

Another situation in which a flash-back may be employed is the following. An actor may read, or relate to some one else, the account of something that has happened to himself or another person. To make this plain to the audience, the incident itself is often shown in the form of a flash-back. An escaped prisoner of war, standing before his own superiors, may tell how he killed the enemy guard in order to make his escape, and the actual killing of the guard may be recalled to the audience by showing a short phase of the struggle during the telling of the story. The music which accompanies the actual scene need not be changed for the moment during which the flash-back lasts; but in order to emphasize the dramatic tension of the incident, the speed and dynamic intensity of the music played should be heightened during the flash-back. In other words, a piece of moderate tempo and moderate loudness played for the scene in which the man appears before the officers, should be played with greater loudness and greater speed while the flash-back lasts, to return instantly to "normal," when the flash-back vanishes.

An instance where perhaps an actual change of music might accompany a flash-back, would be the following. The villain is about to batter in the door of the room in which the heroine is hiding. His brutal efforts and the girl's frenzy are musically depicted by strains of highest emotional and dramatic tension. Meanwhile the hero is furiously riding from a distance, on horseback or by automobile, in order to effect the rescue. During the progress of the main scene, flash-backs are shown of the hero's wild ride. In such an instance it may be admissible to accompany these flash-backs by fast runs on the key-board, with a soft organ registration, increasing in loudness each time that the rider is shown approaching nearer to his goal. When the hero bursts upon the scene, overwhelms the villain and rescues the girl, the climax is reached with a flourish of notes leading into an exalted rendition of the main love theme.

As will be seen by the above, the handling of flash-backs requires a technique of its own; practice will develop it quickly if the underlying principles are correctly understood. These principles are: in most cases *not* to *disrupt* the continuity of the music while the flash-back lasts, but to *change* the *intensity* by playing the music, characteristic of the main action, in a dynamic degree of loudness or softness which befits the secondary action. In a few cases the speed of the music may be changed to advantage, and in rare instances only the flash-back will demand a musical treatment radically differing from that which accompanies the main action. It may be added here that indiscriminately used flash-backs are becoming more and more rare in well-produced pictures, but they are still plentiful in the cheaper films. Flash-backs occur mostly in feature-films, the treatment of which has been described in the preceding chapter.

3. Animated Cartoons and Slap-Stick Comedy

Many a player, who is otherwise admirably fitted to give a musical interpretation of moving pictures, falls down on the animated cartoons and burlesque films. This is due to an absence of the all-important sense of humor, or "comedy touch", which is needed in every-day life as much as in this particular branch of the movie entertainment. Sense of humor is a gift of the gods, but they will not withhold it from any one who seriously tries to acquire it. The player should learn to recognize, and be able personally to enjoy, the fun of the comic situations depicted on the screen. Nothing is more calamitous than to see "Mutt and Jeff" disport themselves in their inimitable antics and to have a "Brother Gloom" at the organ who gives vent to his perennial grouch in sadly sentimental or funereal strains. A cheerful aspect of things, the faculty to laugh with and at the world, are indispensable. In no part of the pictures should the attention of the player be riveted more firmly on the screen than here. If the "point" of the joke be missed, if the player lag behind with his effect, all will be lost, and the audience cheated out of its rightful share of joy. Nor does it suffice, as seems to be the idea of certain picture-players, to be armed with one lively tune that must serve all cartoons, comedies and jokes, invariably and indiscriminately. In the cartoons and in the comedies all sorts of other emotions, besides that of plain hilarity, may come into play; there may be sorrow, doubt, horror and even death; only all these emotions lack the quality of truth, and they must be expressed as "mock" sorrow and grief, "mock" doubt and death. This is very different from reality and should therefore be treated differently in the music. Take as a glaring example the funeral march of Chopin, with its sublime note of tragedy and bereavement, and the exquisite "Funeral March for a Marionette" by Gounod, with its suggestion of fine persiflage. This method, applied to the most serious situation, can naturally be adapted to any other emotion that the player may encounter in a legitimate picture drama and that he will have to "caricature" for the picture farce.

Nowhere does success, the "getting across" of a picture, depend so much on special effects as it does here. It may be stated candidly that these effects, and the best among them, are not always purely musical. As will be pointed out in the chapter on "Special Effects," a battery of traps and other accessories are really needed to emphasize in a comic manner the action on the screen. It is often noise, more than music, that is wanted, to arouse the hilarity of the audience; and the noise again may be of various kinds. It should always be broadly imitative when accompanying a fall, a hit, a slide, a whirl or flight through the air, a brawl, the whistle of an engine, the chirping of a bird, the mewing of a cat, or the barking of a dog. In the last analysis it takes very little to make a crowd laugh; only the fuse to its magazine of laughter must be ignited with a live spark. Experience, here as in everything else, will prove the best teacher, and the player will soon find out what effects work best and produce the surest results.

This part of the show is admirably adapted to the introduction of all sorts of popular songs and dances. The player should keep in touch with the publications of popular music houses, since it will repay him to establish a reputation which will make the public say: "Let's go to the Star Theatre — you always hear the latest tune there." This will prove a never-failing drawing card for the younger generation of movie-fans, and it will react most decidedly to the advantage of the organist in his relation to the box-office and his own earning power.

It is well also to keep in touch with the monthly announcements of the latest phonograph records issued. As a rule, these numbers have proved assured successes, and people like to hear their favorite tunes, either those they already have at home, or new ones which they might want to add to their collection. The player's repertoire should always be kept alive by the infusion of new and up-to-date material.

One important factor in these pictorial farces is the matter of speed. "Pep" is the key-note to the situation, with the current "jazz" tunes as a medium. When special effects are to be introduced, or certain moods and emotions are to be "italicized" and burlesqued, this may be done at any point of the composition played, the piece instantly to be resumed. Above all, keep things "going," like a juggler who may be handling two or twenty balls, and occasionally drops one, but must never cease in throwing and catching something.[1]

4. THE COMEDY DRAMA

Much that has been said in the previous chapter also applies to this type of film. However, all effects, in general, will have to be toned down and the methods employed will approach more nearly those of the "feature film." Sense of humor should again be the chief asset of the player. But it should be rather a sense of wit than a fondness for horse-play. Fine musical taste, a light touch, apt musical illustrations, will greatly add to the charm of the picture.

The player will here, as in the feature film, characterize the chief actors by suitable motives; there will be a main theme and the obligatory

---

[1] Such pieces as "The Bim-Bims" by Adam, "Lydia" by Fomin, "Donkey Trot" by Leducq, "La Gloria" by Densmore, "With Xylophone and Bells" and "The Juggler Comedian" by Huerter, "On the Hike" by Dumas, "Polka Humoristique" by Lacomb, and "Chatterbox" by d'Ambrosio will prove useful material. The player should have at his command the choruses of such well-known topical songs as "I cannot make my eyes behave," "Every little movement has a meaning all its own," "Where did you get that hat?" "Always go while the going is good," "Waiting at the Church," "What's the matter with Father?" "My mind's made up to marry Carolina," etc., etc. The association of such tunes with their particular text phrase will always insure a quick response in the audience, if the tunes are applied to the proper situation.

number of supplementary selections. As there is usually a love story interwoven, there will be need of some sentimental strain besides pieces of a lighter nature. For flights, escapes and chases, the player should hold in readiness various kinds of musical "hurries." [1] A notable feature of the comedy drama is the "comic mystery," which should be as distinct from the heavy mystery of the tragic drama as is the funeral march of Gounod from that by Chopin, alluded to in the preceding chapter. To obtain a good "mock mystery," the "comedy touch" and dramatic instinct must work hand in hand.

The player, alas, will soon discover that there are many so-called comedy dramas shown which are hopelessly dull and barren of action or interest. In such cases, the only thing for the player to do, is to give a quasi-organ-recital of light and graceful music (no fugues or sonatas!), and to atone by the merit of his playing for the faults of the film.

In a city where musical shows are produced at the legitimate theatres, the player will do well to use selections from such productions, just playing, in the accompaniment to the lighter picture dramas.

5. WEEKLY NEWS PICTURES

The topical character of these pictures calls, as a rule, for topical music. The audience that fills a moving picture house likes to hear the popular success of the hour, be it a song or instrumental number, well played and effectively rendered. It goes without saying, that due regard must always be exercised in instances where the music and picture might clash. It will never do to launch forth on a popular dance tune which might fit one scene, showing some public happenings with which this music might agree, and to persist in playing the tune while the picture shifts to the scene of a funeral or disaster. But, as a general rule, the news section of the picture is the one that will give the best opportunity to play the lighter type of popular numbers.

Unless the picture is of such character that it would call for a specially appropriate musical illustration, the tune need not be changed for every scene that is shown. But there are certain events, of which we shall speak in the following paragraphs, that should receive special musical treatment.

Military or civic processions will require martial music. Pictures of weddings might be emphasized by a strain from Mendelssohn's or de Koven's wedding music. A funeral procession should be accompanied by the playing of Chopin's or Beethoven's funeral march. This will also be appropriate for the showing of graves or a cemetery.

---

[1] Grieg's "In the Hall of the Mountain King" is particularly useful as a comedy agitato.

Church functions will suggest the playing of a chorale or some well-known sacred music. Patriotic gatherings or the showing of statesmen and royal personages should be accompanied by patriotic music or by the national anthem of the particular country whose statesman or ruler is shown. It is against the law to play garbled versions of "The Star Spangled Banner" or paraphrase on it. If played at all, our national anthem should be given in its entirety, with spirited movement and yet in a dignified manner. However, the anthem should not be dragged in without rhyme or reason, perhaps simply because the flag is displayed in some picture. Since the audience will rise whenever the anthem is played, it should be introduced, if at all, not more than once at each performance, and only when the scene demands it.

The player should familiarize himself with the most important and common bugle signals of the Army. There are many occasions where these bugle signals will add a dramatic touch. If the picture shows a military funeral or the graves of soldiers, the signal of "taps" should be played in a suitable register, first unaccompanied, to imitate the bugle, and then, if the picture offers an opportunity, the player may improvise on the bugle call as a motive.

Frequently pictures of aëroplanes and other air-craft are thrown on the screen. These should be accompanied by light, "soaring" music (such as "Through Space" by Paul Wachs or "Butterfly Chase" by Hugo Argus). If an aëroplane makes a rapid and spectacular descent, the player might lightly glide his thumb down the keys.

Horse races or automobile races call for rapid music. If the player's technique is not sufficiently developed to execute a generally difficult composition that demands a great deal of speed, he may obtain satisfactory results by a rapid *tremolo* in the treble, punctuated by crisp chord progressions, of moderate speed, played in a lower register. In any event, the player must approximate the speed of the picture, and communicate to the audience the excitement and tension that the original witnesses of the scene must have felt. Football games may call for college songs. Other sportive happenings, such as baseball or tennis, seldom require special music. It is different with boat races or sailing regattas. They should not only be accompanied by music suggestive of the speed, but also of the graceful movement of the sailing boats, or of the swell of the sea. Waltzes are very appropriate for yachting scenes.

Fire scenes demand music of dramatic excitement, interspersed with *glissandi* (slides) on the keys, from bass to treble, to illustrate the leaping flames. If the fire increases or decreases in violence, the player should suggest this in his music. Should the flames become extinguished, and the scene show the rack and ruin of the place, the music should calm down and express the mournful desolation of the picture.

For launching of boats, it is advisable to add to the tension of the picture by accompanying the sliding of the boat along the ways with an appropriate tremolo in the treble, immediately breaking into a joyous tune of a "horn-pipe" character, when the boat takes the water. The player will find it useful to familiarize himself with a number of chanties or sailor songs, as they will fit in not only with "news" pictures, but in a great many feature films.

In the showing of industrial plants where hammering and the clangor of machines dominate, such pieces as the "Anvil Chorus" will often add to the enjoyment of the audience. Pictures of agricultural scenes might fittingly be accompanied by some of the "rural" songs and dances that the audience is familiar with. Scenes in the South, cotton fields, steamers on the Mississippi, etc., etc., will call for the songs of Stephen Foster, Virginia reels, Negro spirituals, etc.

Events in foreign lands, if these lands are in the Orient, will take on added significance in the minds of the audience, if they are accompanied by music which suggests Oriental strains (such as "Orientale" by J. R. Manzanares, "Orientale" by C. Cui, "Koko-San" by I. Kamoto; see also "From Russia" by G. Borch, "Nochecita" by I. Albeniz, "Spanish Serenade" by Strelezki, "Italian Serenade" by S. Maykapar, etc., etc.).[1]

Under the heading of "news" pictures, are often run films that portray the latest fashions. Such exhibitions require no special music. They call for agreeable and fluent salon music, or waltzes (see "Iris" by R. Friml, "Fleur-de-lis" by J. Martel, "In the Starlight" by C. Huerter, "Ecstasy" by S. Baynes, etc.).

6. EDUCATIONAL FILMS

More than any other pictures, educational films should absorb the whole attention of the spectators. By their very nature and purpose, they are intended to impart information or instruction of a general or special order. The music that accompanies such views should therefore be carefully calculated not to distract the attention. The player should avoid loud or showy pieces, and instead play music that will be conducive to the creation of a calm and receptive mood in the listener.

---

[1] The player will find a great many pieces of general usefulness and special applicability to national events in the series of volumes, published in the Boston Music Company Edition, and containing representative pieces of various national schools. So far, the series comprises the following countries: America, France, Russia, Scandinavia, Italy, Germany, Bohemia (Slovak countries), Spain and Finland.

The organ registration for such pieces should be soft, nor should it be too changeful, but rather adhere to one and the same registration for some length of time.

There may be certain views, however, which by virtue of a musical emphasis will tell their lesson more vividly. In the showing of growth and development of flowers or insects, a crescendo that follows the progress of the picture might not be out of place. Certain views of animal life may suggest to the player particular effects that will be in keeping with the story told on the screen. Scientific demonstrations rarely call for special effects.

The case is different, when the education is to be imparted by means of travel pictures. These require a few words of special advice.

7. TRAVEL VIEWS

In dealing with travel views the player should bear in mind, first of all, that he must provide his memory or his stock of accessible music with a number of pieces that are directly intended by their composers as nature studies, more or less sharply defining certain moods on land and sea, or will do so by implication. The well-stocked library of a picture player should contain various categories of music, catalogued according to the applicability of each piece, with plenty of cross references so that at a moment's notice the player·may lay his hand on the desired composition. For travel views he may find it convenient to order his music according to 1, nature in general, and 2, special countries, with a possible addition of 3, particular occupations or situations.

Under the head of "Nature in General" would come 1, landscapes and 2, water scenes. The first of these may appear in three general aspects; namely, 1, sunny, 2, cloudy, and 3, stormy. Music will be found that will fit more intimately the views of placid gardens and orchards, harmonize with undulating fields, shady woods, rugged mountains, or majestic glaciers. In each case, a certain affinity between the music and the· pictured scene should be sought.

There exists a great deal of music that by its very name suggests woodland scenes, or quaint gardens (see especially the works of MacDowell, Nevin, or Grieg).

"Water scenes," on the other hand, may differentiate between views of brooks, lakes, rivers, or oceans. Here, again, any number of compositions with suggestive titles will give the player ample material to choose from. A frequent occurrence is the showing of cascades or rapids. These lend themselves admirably to musical illustration by means of brilliant arpeggios or purling runs.   The seascape, in turn, may be shown in a state of utter calm, of moderate motion, or lashed by a storm.   Each will require a different musical treatment.

While it is difficult to give a complete catalogue of music that will embrace all possible travel pictures, the following suggestions will at least serve to call the player's attention to some of the scenes he is likely to encounter. He will do well to reckon with these possibilities and to fix in his mind certain musical subjects that he will always have available, at short notice.

Among the pictures of the U. S. A. the player will have to reckon with Southern scenes (negro activities, etc.), which will call for tunes that are typical of the South, such as the songs of Stephen Foster and others. The West will furnish pictures of cowboys, round-ups, mining activities, mountain scenes, etc., which may be made more graphic by the playing of music that approximates the particular situation.   Coast scenes will generally demand music that in some way suggests the water.   From the North you may expect views of winter sports, such as skating, skiing, or ice-boating.   The player should know a number of typically American songs and tunes, representative of various States and races.

The Orient, in general, furnishes a limited type of views.   There are processions, temple scenes, dances, fête days, and the like.   The player should command over a fairly representative repertoire of exotic strains, some typical of Arabia and Persia, some of India, others of China and Japan. There are distinct differences between the music of these countries, and an earnest student of the subject will try to find something characteristic of each of them.   It is here, in particular, that the player may exert a great educative influence on the audience.   Rather gloomy and monotonous music will befit the desert, while brilliant and scintillating music should accompany the hustle and bustle of Oriental street scenes and bazaars. As a rule, Oriental music is distinguished rather by a peculiar inflection of the melody than by variety of harmonic treatment.   The latter belongs to the Occident.   Therefore it will often suffice if the player adheres for his accompaniment to a droning bass of either an open fifth or fourth, or a stereotyped rhythmical figure that is indicative of either the languor of the scene (opium dens, harems, etc.) or of its typical movement (Arabian caravans, Oriental dancers, Chinese junks).   A few works may be suggested here, as offering a great deal of useful material of distinctly Oriental color, such as "Scheherazade" by Rimsky-Korsakov (for Persian-Arabian motives), the opera "Lakme" by Delibes and the ballet "Namouna" by Lalo (for East Indian and Arabian motives), "Caucasian Sketches" by Ippolitov-Iwanov (for motives from Asiatic Russia), the opera "Madame Butterfly" by Puccini (for Japanese motives), the piano suites "Dreamer's Tales" and "Betel, Jade and Ivory" by Peterkin (for Chinese and Malay themes). There are, of course, a great many other works that would come into consideration, such as "Scenes in Algeria" by Saint-Saëns, African Suites by Coleridge Taylor; but it would lead too far to give a complete enumeration, and it must be left to the zeal of the player to find additional material that he may require.

It may be well to remind the player with what variety of scenes in views of Europe he may meet. He will do well to carry in his memory some of the well-known folk-songs of England, Scotland, and Ireland, folk-dances of Italy and Spain, folk-tunes of Russia and Scandinavia, and some characteristic songs of France. It will not do always to play the national anthems of such countries except when really national events are shown. For travel pictures the folk-song literature of these countries should be drawn upon.[1]

---

[1] Much useful music will be found in the volumes of various national schools contained in the Boston Music Company Edition and mentioned in footnote on page 40.

PART III

THE THEATRICAL ORGAN

1. Peculiarities of Organ Technique

The difficulties peculiar to playing on and handling of the *organ* as distinguished from the *pianoforte* may be classified as follows:

a. How to sit at the organ.

b. Pedalling (playing with the feet).

c. Independence of movement between hands and feet, separately and in combination.

d. Use of *legato* and *staccato* touch.

e. Registration (management of stops and various mechanical appliances).

Fluent piano technique is the first requisite for a successful theatrical organist. Assuming that the candidate possesses this, coupled with expert sight-reading ability and a talent for improvising, he is ready for the work.

a. *How to sit at the organ*

This is perhaps the most important item of a theatrical organist's equipment, since he must contend with long hours and physical strain.

Seat yourself in the *middle* of the bench (and stay there). Now lift up both feet and hold them over the pedals, with the tips of the boots over the black keys and the heels over the white, at *the same time* holding both hands over the manuals (keyboards for the hands) ready to play. Move the hands and feet in the air. If you have an uncomfortable sensation that you are going to fall off or tip over, the bench is too far away from the keys or, most likely of all, you are sitting too near its edge. Try the bench at different distances from the keyboard until you find the right spot where by sitting erectly and well back *on* the bench, using the end of the spine as the center of motion, not (barrel hoop fashion) the middle of the back, you can swing arms and legs freely and yet reach the various manuals with ease. Arrange your music at the proper distance from your eyes, and you are

44

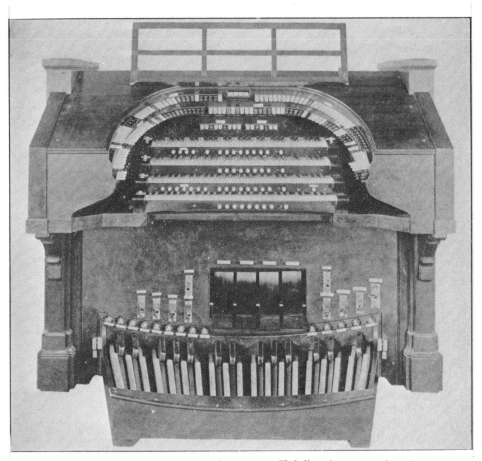

FOUR–MANUAL ORGAN CONSOLE ("Unit" orchestra type)

ready to play.   In most of the theatres, the organ bench is provided with a back.   This is an absolute necessity in playing long hours.   But do not forget that the bench must be properly placed, just the same; fit the bench to the body and not the body to the bench.   The failure to sit correctly brings endless physical strain, even induces serious ailments, particularly with women players.   For the unpleasant arm fatigue encountered in playing too long on the upper manuals of a three or four manual organ, a remedy is found in coupling through to one of the lower manuals, which is explained farther on.

Right here be it said that every excess or unnecessary movement of the arms and legs is so much energy thrown away.   There are organists and pianists who have acquired an unhappy "futurist" style of performance by throwing the hands in the air at the end of a (to them) thrilling passage, waving the body, shaking the head — all of which is so much electricity gone to waste.   The man who sits in absolute repose before his organ, perfectly balanced, muscles relaxed and easy, with no hifalutin motions, is the man who is going to last the longest and produce the most virile and forceful music.

b. *Pedalling*

Wear round-toed, medium-heeled shoes, with flexible soles, not too thin.

The pedals are played by means of the heel and toes.   (The flat of the foot is used only when a group of two or three "black" keys are encountered, viz: C♯, D♯; F♯, G♯, A♯, or B♭, A♭, G♭; E♭, D♭.) This means that a flexible ankle is of the utmost importance.   The leg, contrary to general notions, is not used except as a means of carrying the foot to the desired position.   The actual playing of the pedals begins at the ankle.   This is a principle similar to that which governs piano playing, a loose wrist being there the first requisite, as is a loose ankle in organ pedalling.

Place the foot in position, press down the toe and then the heel, and so on, alternating toe and heel; when the toe goes down the heel is released, when the heel is pressed down the toes are released, using a free ankle as the center of action.

Should the ankle be allowed to become stiff and rigid, the weight of the *whole leg* will be used to drive the sole of the foot against the pedal keys, resulting in the destruction or injury of the pedal mechanism and most certainly rendering absolutely impossible the performance of rapid pedal passages.

Do not look at the pedal board while playing.

Having seated yourself correctly in the centre of the bench, prepared to *stay in the centre*, you are ready to learn to "feel with your toes" — viz, play without looking at the feet.   Locate the spaces between the groups of short keys.   They correspond exactly to the open space between the groups of black keys on the piano — B♭ and C♯ — E♭ and F♯.

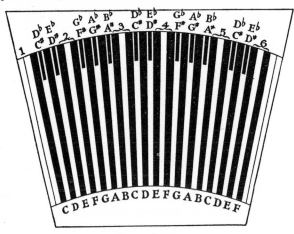

PEDAL-BOARD

Thrust the foot into the space marked 2 in the drawing, the toes will then be over the ends of E and F ; then into the spaces marked 3, 4, etc.

Having thus located these spaces, the adjoining " black " keys are easily found.   This method of feeling for the whereabouts of the notes until one's feet by long habit go there of their own accord, is the same as that of a blind man first learning to play the piano.   He must perforce feel for the spaces between the black keys and then get his bearings.

There are various books of pedal exercise which can be used in practicing ; or the average musician can easily improvise his own exercises, using those intervals most often encountered in his own work.

c. *Independence of movement between hands and feet, separately and in combination*

For the theatrical organist, this is of prime importance, since the *left hand* comes into a special realm of its own in this work.   Practice playing all tunes with the left hand, making them "sing" as they would if played by the right hand.   Then try playing any tune you desire with the left hand, with expression, and in strict time, in the meantime playing a chromatic scale up and down another manual.   After this can be done, make the right hand more elaborate, playing arpeggios of various kinds. Finally try playing an entirely different tune with the right hand, keeping both tunes going at once, each complete in itself.   When this can be done (which will not be in a day or a week) add a pedal obbligato ; *i.e.* a bass melody, or play the tune on the pedals, an obbligato with the left hand and variations with the right hand.

When practicing scales on the pedals, *always* play a scale with the left hand at the same time, in contrary motion to the one you are practicing on the pedals. This serves to break the "invisible wire" that seems to run down your left arm through your left leg. It also serves as a guard against getting out of position on the bench.

When reaching for notes at the end of the pedal-board, do not slide along the bench, but instead, turn the body as little as necessary, the end of the spine as a pivot.

d. *Staccato and legato touch*

Theatrical work is the antithesis of church playing. A crisp, clean staccato (detached) touch is the first requisite. Most everything is played staccato, except for special effects, such as the main love theme, church scenes, or similar situations for which a legato (connected) touch is wanted.

The best pattern that can be followed is the *orchestra*. Make use of every opportunity to listen to an orchestra. Watch the attacks, releases and styles of playing of the different instruments, solo and ensemble. Especially try to get the general effect of the concerted staccato and legato. By carefully listening to the good theatrical orchestras travelling with good opera and musical comedy companies, an entire course of instruction in itself may be had in this manner; not only instruction in touch and style, but also in tonal coloring, or "registration."

e. *Registration*

(Management of the stops and various mechanical appliances, combination of stops, etc.)

Here, again, the theatrical organist must be an orchestra director and arranger in thought and spirit. Go to the orchestra for your tonal effects and combinations.

Many ideas concerning registration can be gained by playing from " conductor's " (or piano) parts of orchestrations, and by substituting for the " cues " the organ stops corresponding to the instruments designated. The following will be a guide to such " orchestral " registration.

2. " ORCHESTRATION " BY MEANS OF ORGAN STOPS

As a rule, the tone-quality of a stop is indicated by its name; *i.e.* Flute, Trumpet, Oboe, Violin, etc.

The pitch of the stop is indicated by numerals, placed after its name; *i.e.* Flute 8′, Bourdon 16′, Piccolo 2′, Viol 4′.

8′ (meaning "eight-foot tone") indicates that the key struck will sound *unison pitch*, or the same as it would if struck on the piano. This pitch is produced by a pipe 8 ft. in *length*.

A pipe of 4′, proportionately formed, will sound notes *one octave higher* than one of 8′.

So also a pipe of 16′ will produce a tone *one octave lower* than one of 8′; similarly a pipe of 2′ will sound *two octaves above* one of 8′, etc.

Stops of 8′ (or unison pitch), 4′, or 2′ are called "Foundation" stops, unless specially voiced for solo use.

Stops of 5′ 4″ (5 feet 4 inches) and 2′ 8″ are called "Mutation" stops, because the pipes of these stops sound a pitch other than that of unison or its octaves.

Stops having several pipes to each note are called "Compound" stops or are more generally known as "Mixtures."

The following is a list of stops likely to be encountered on a journey from a small two-manual to a large four-manual theatrical organ. Every organ builder has his own ideas in the matter of stop nomenclature, but the name generally gives some indication as to the tone-quality. The stops have been classified according to their orchestral usefulness, and not divided into "organs," with the idea in mind that having once learned the meaning of the various names, the player will be able to identify the stops with ease, no matter where he may find them. In these days of "duplex" organ building, one is never sure to find certain stops on the same manuals.

The manuals (or "organs") are usually arranged in the following order:

1. Solo
2. Swell
3. Great
4. Orchestral (choir)

Small organs always lack the first manual, and sometimes also the fourth. The stops are either in the form of draw-knobs at the sides, or in rows of ivory tablets at the top, just above the upper manual, as indicated in the various illustrations. In the use of draw-stops, the "coupler" tablets are generally placed above. These "couplers" are mechanical devices whereby the stops in any one manual may be added to any other manual. Thus by turning down the tablet marked "Swell to Great" we can play on the Great manual and yet have any or all of the Swell stops at our command. When the prolonged playing on an upper manual becomes irksome, shut off all orchestral stops from the orchestral manual and couple the "Swell to Orchestral," and you have your "Swell" manual moved down several inches.

These couplers are only used for joining less to greater, thus: Swell to Orchestral, Swell to Great, Orchestral to Great — never Great to Swell. A list of "couplers" will be found at the end of the enumeration of stops.

MANUAL STOPS

FOUNDATION STOPS

	Voix Céleste	
	Salicional (Salicet)	
	Dulciana	
	Keraulophon	
	Gamba	
	Viol de Gamba	
	Gemshorn	Strings
	Dolce	
	Aeoline	
	Geigen Principal	
	Dulcet	
	Viol d'amour	
	Stopped Diapason	
8' tone	Lieblich Gedackt	
	Rohrflöte	
	Grosse Flöte (great flute)	
	Doppel Flöte (double flute)	
	Harmonic Flute	
	Melodia	Wood wind
	Waldflöte (woodland flute)	
	Flauto Dolce (sweet flute)	
	Concert Flute	
	Clarabella	
	Clarinet	
	Saxophone	
	Small Open Diapason	Organ tone
	Large Open Diapason	
	Gemshorn (Alpine horn)	
	Salicet	Strings
	Viol d'amour	
4' tone	Flute Harmonique	
	Waldflöte	Wood wind
	Flute d'amour	
	Principal, or Octave	Organ tone

2' tone
- Piccolo (small flute)
- Flageolet or Flautina
- Gemshorn (Alpine horn)
- Fifteenth or Super-Octave

} Wood wind

REED STOPS

16' tone
- Contra-Hautboy
- Contra-Fagotto
- Contra-Posaune
- Ophicleide

} Correspond to the brass choir in orchestra

8' tone
- Oboe (orchestral)
- Bassoon
- Oboe or Hautboy
- English Horn

} Same tone as their prototypes in orchestra

- Vox Humana   Imitation of the human voice

- French Horn
- Trumpet
- Tuba Mirabilis
- Horn
- Cornopean
- Posaune

} Brass choir

4' tone   Clarion   Very brilliant, flaring brass

MUTATION STOPS

5' 4" — Quint
2' 8" — Twelfth, or Octave-Quint
2'   — Fifteenth

COMPOUND STOPS

Each stop having several pipes to each note
- Echo cornet
- Sesquialtera
- Mixture
- Sharp Mixture

These stops, combining several tones in one, add richness and brilliancy. They vary in different organs as to tonal power, *i.e.* forte or piano, and must be experimented with. The tone-quality, generally speaking, of compound stops is that of the wood-wind section of the orchestra.

The following will give some idea of the sound of these stops:

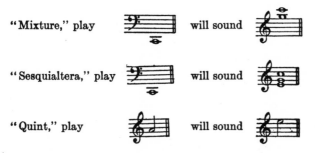

"Mixture," play   [musical notation]   will sound   [musical notation]

"Sesquialtera," play   [musical notation]   will sound   [musical notation]

"Quint," play   [musical notation]   will sound   [musical notation]

"Fifteenth," sounding fifteen above the key struck.

Double Stops

Of 16-foot length or tone	Double-stopped Diapason 16′ Bourdon Double-open Diapason	No duplicate in orchestra. Soft & sweet, cloying if used too much. Full, rich organ tone.

Pedal Stops

The important distinction between stops on the Pedal Organ and those on the Manuals is that the former are uniformly one octave lower in pitch. Thus, as the Open Diapason of a Manual is of 8′ tone, the Open Diapason on the Pedal Organ will be of 16′; also, as the Double stops of the manuals are of 16′ tone, those of the pedals are 32′.

Foundation Stops

16′ tone	Bourdon *ff*	Smooth, full tone; disturbing if used too much.
	Bourdon *pp*	Soft and generally useful.
	Violone	Excellent imitation of contrabass in orchestra.
	Open Diapason *mf* Open Diapason *ff*	Full, open organ tone.
	Dulciana Gamba	Light string tone, duplexed from manuals.
8′ tone	Flute Violoncello Octave	Correspond to same stops on manuals. Rather assertive quality when used in pedal.

Reed Stops

32′ length	Contra-Posaune Bombarde Contra-Fagotto	Brass choir; corresponding to the giant tubas seen occasionally in orchestras
16′ length	Fagotto Trombone Posaune Ophicleide Tuba	Brass choir
8′ length	Tuba	Brass choir
4′ length	Clarion	Brass choir

Double Stops

32′ tone	Sub-bass or Double-stopped Diapason or Contra-Bourdon Diapason Violone	Used in combination. Only for special effects. Typically organistic — not orchestral.

Couplers

Swell to Swell 4′ — (super-octave)   Great to Great, 4′
Swell to Swell 16′ — (sub-octave)   Great to Great, 16′

Swell to Great
Swell to Great 4'
Swell to Great 16'
Swell to Orchestral
Swell to Orchestral 4'
Swell to Orchestral 16'
Swell to Solo

Orchestral to Orchestral
Orchestral to Orchestral 4'
Orchestral to Orchestral 16'
Orchestral to Great
Orchestral to Great 4'
Orchestral to Great 16'
Orchestral to Solo

Solo to Solo 4'
Solo to Solo 16'
Solo to Great

Swell to Pedal
Great to Pedal
Orchestral to Pedal
Solo to Pedal

PISTONS

The little buttons underneath each manual are called "pistons" and are numbered 1, 2, 3, 4, etc.   By means of a board inside the organ or, on the newer organs, at the organ desk, different combinations of stops may be "set up" and locked under each of these pistons so that by pushing a certain button with the thumb an entirely new set of stops may be had in a fraction of time and effort.   It is always safest to have the organ-tuner show you how to work the various mechanical devices on a strange organ.

3. SWELL PEDALS AND CRESCENDO PEDAL

Swell Pedals

Just above the pedal keys will be found two, three, or four, balanced pedals the size of a foot which control the volume of tone emitted from the various manuals.   Usually the Solo is farthest to the *left*, the Orchestral and Great next, being combined in one, then that of the Swell organ, with the *Crescendo* pedal on the *right*.

Learn to use the swell pedals with either foot.   Watch the constant light and shade of the orchestra and try to imitate this, always careful not to exaggerate.   Do not thrust the swell pedals all the way in, every time.   By experimenting and listening to your own playing, you will soon find that just a little "*crescendo*" or "*diminuendo*" is quite sufficient, and more effective than a complete *pp* $\longrightarrow$ *fff* $\longrightarrow$ *pp*.   A continuous performance on this principle will soon find the audience in a delightfully bewildered state of mind, bordering on nausea, caused by "weathering" too many "tonal waves."

Crescendo Pedal

This pedal is either a great blessing or a great nuisance, according to the use to which you put it.   By means of it, the organist can, with a minimum of effort, merely by pressing the foot, throw on consecutively, as regards increase of tonal power, all the stops in the organ.   The trouble lies in this very fact: ease of manipulation.   It is so easy to keep the foot on this pedal, working it back and forth without thought or reason, instead of studying out stop combinations, usually keeping it at the *full organ,* which is the motion picture organist's greatest bugbear: playing *too loud.*

The main use of the crescendo pedal in theatrical playing is for *sforzando* effects and orchestral *accent.*   By placing the whole foot firmly on this pedal, controlling it by a turn of the ankle, an instant crash to *fff* and back again to the *p* combination already set up on the organ, may be accomplished without harm to the instrument.   Stabbing at the end of the pedal with a thrust of the boot will jar the mechanism out of order.

This pedal is of course useful in building up long *crescendo* effects, but these sustained effects are not so much encountered in theatrical work, the effect here being accomplished more by individual tone color than volume of sound.

4. The Identification of Tone-colors for Descriptive Purposes
(Registration)

The term "tone-color" is a compound, linking conceptions that belong to two different arts, which are music and painting.   It is the simplest way of describing certain qualities that tone possesses, qualities which enable it to assume different hues and shadings, as it were.   The painter has at his disposal many colors, from which he chooses those particular to the scene that he is depicting, selecting always such modifications of each color as will express the very atmosphere that he wishes to give to his picture. In this way we will find that the painter has at his disposal varying shades of red, different tints of blue, greens which contain more yellow and others which border on the black.   The Papal manufacture of mosaics in Rome differentiates actually between a little over 25,000 distinct color variations. Tone-color, to be sure, is not able to take on such a formidable number of gradations, but there are enough to give it a wide range of different qualities which will react differently upon the listener.

It should be remembered that tone-color proper is one of the three fundamental characteristics that constitute musical sounds, the other two being pitch and intensity.   Therefore the term tone-color should not be mistaken for any one of the two others.   A given tone-color may be applied to musical sounds of different pitch, high and low, and of different intensities, loud or soft.

The following table will serve as first aid in "registration" or the use of organ-stops (tone-colors) either singly or in combination.

For "Neutral" Scenes (no emotion) scenery; action having no definite intensity; views from an aëroplane (when the hum of the motor is the only sound) or views from a great height.   Also (see special effects) wind, rain, etc. }   String tones, 16', 8', 4,' 2', as solo with accompaniment and in 4-pt. harmony.

For Specific Emotions, Moods, and Situations.

Love . . . .   solo flute 4' — acc. of strings or harp. } light pedal
close harmony strings 16', 8', 4', 2' and Vox Humana.
saxophone solo — strings 8', flute 8' accompaniment.

Happiness
  Springtime, sunshine .   flutes, 16', 8', 4', 2' and strings.
Joy . . . .   same as above, intensified in volume by coupling the various manuals together.
Hope . . . .   flute 8' — string acc.
Victory . . . . . .   full organ.
Exaltation . . . . .   organ tone, rising to full organ.
Prayer . . . . . .   solo flute 8' or Vox Humana 4-pt. harmony.
Church scenes . . . .   organ tone, coupled & heavy Ped.
Impressive dignity . .   organ tone, coupled & heavy Ped.
Suspicion . . . . .   clarinet solo with string acc.
Entreaty . . . . .   saxophone solo with string 8' and flute 8' acc.
Yearning . . . . .   Vox Humana solo with string 16', 8', 4', 2' acc.
Anxiety . . . . . .   full string choir and Vox Humana in 4-pt. harmony — tremolo.
Temptation . . . .   clarinet or oboe with string acc.
Hatred . . . . . .   soft toned reeds gradually increasing in volume of tone to climax.
Suspense and impending disaster . . . . .   The clarinet alone or any flute that is a near approach to an orchestral French horn when used as solo, alone, and without the tremulant; use a string acc. tremolo.
Defiance . . . . . .   reeds *mf*.
Treachery . . . . .   reeds *mf*.
Rage . . . .   reeds, varying the volume of tone according to the intensity of the mood.
Cruelty . . . . .   reed (Cornopean) either as solo and strings 16', 8', 4', 2' with double st. Diap. 16' as acc. or in 4-pt. harmony.
Torture . . . . . .   reeds *f*.
Grief . . . .   oboe or clarinet solo, string and flute acc. or full string choir and Vox Humana.
Despair . . . . . .   clarinet solo.
Passion . . . . . .   reed solo played in lower octaves, strings, flute 8' and clarinet as accompaniment, *mf* pedal.
Renunciation . . . .   Vox Humana or mellow flute 8' played in lower octaves of keyboard — no pedal.
Dreaming . . . .   string choir 16', 8', 4', 2', and harp.   Very light pedal.

NATURE SCENES

Shimmering water . . string choir 16', 8', 4', 2' in upper octaves with harp arpeggios as acc. Very light pedal.

Birds singing . . . . Flute Harmonique 4' or piccolo 2'.

Morning (Dawn) . . . flute 4' as solo — strings tremolo acc.; no pedal (increasing in intensity as dawn spreads, beginning *pp.* with crescendo to full organ, if sun bursts forth).

Night . . . . . . mellow flute without tremulant played 4-pt. harmony in lower octaves — no pedal.

COMEDY . . . . . . flutes 8', 4', coupled to oboe 16' and piccolo 2' as solo, with flute and string acc., played staccato and at a lively tempo, make a bright setting. Use light pedal. The heavy Doppel Flöte or Grosse Flöte can be used in burlesque effect, staccato, glissando, etc. For "jazz" effects, use strings 8', 4', and clarinet in right hand acc., "jazzing" with the left hand, using saxophone, or heavy flute and saxophone with an assertive but not too heavy pedal. The xylophone is always used as a solo. Use xylophone and piccolo 2', or xylophone, clarinet, flute 4' with string 8' and flute 8' accompaniment, light pedal.

TENSION

Agitatos ("hurries") mobs, horse-races, wild-west scenes, fights, pursuits.

These numbers should be characterized first by their rhythm and tempo. The tone-coloring is according to the mood — joy, suspense, hatred, etc. A pedal cadenza often adds to the climax of a fight, mob scene, etc.

falls . . . . . . Sudden opening and closing of the Crescendo Pedal.

crashes . . . . . All of the above effects are intensified or lessened by the swell pedals, controlling the volume of tone.

MISTERIOSO

Scenes of mystery, or suppressed alarm, sinister forebodings, ghost scenes, supernatural apparitions, etc.

Softest strings tremolo, and as the situation grows more tense the music should rather become softer than louder, yet the movement and the mood must be sustained. The tremolo will be most effective if the speed is accelerated, while the volume of tone is lessened. Immediately before the climax, it is well to go into a recitative, however short, ushering in the climax either by means of an absolute silence (in cases of horror or in the presence of tragedy) or by a *sforzando* chord leading into the proper motive (in cases of victory or successful dénouement of the tension).

RECITATIVE

For scenes as mentioned above under misterioso, for scenes of superlative tension.

The quality of the recitative must always be dramatic, that is, it must be expressive of the proper mood which it is to portray, either horror or mystery or suspense. Samples of recitatives may be found in a great many operas where they are employed, particularly in passages where the dramatic action progresses quickly. To convey the appropriate color, make use of the "uncanny" registers of the clarinet and bassoon stops; for cruelty, a coarse reed such as the Cornopean will prove useful.

The player will often find moments when, on first seeing a picture, the development of the story will leave him puzzled; rather than make a misstep, he will do well to abide his time by means of a short recitative, until the trend of events becomes obvious.

There are situations in comedy dramas and in farces where an occasional recitative will be most fitting; naturally, the treatment of the recitative itself, as well as organ stop employed, should emphasize the humor of the situation. The use of a heavy flute in a burlesque fashion will depict ludicrous antics, and that of a light screechy reed may be easily manipulated to indicate gossiping women, etc.

Avoid constant use of too heavy pedal tone! Nothing gets on the nerves of the audience quicker than the ever present deep rumble of the pedal. Use pedal 8' rather than pedal 16', and learn to use it as part of the harmony, not just hop toad fashion with the left foot, such as this,

but treat the bass as the foundation of the harmony and as an independently *moving voice,* such as

or, for a march time, in the style of the following:

5. Special Effects, and How to Produce Them

The best, and the only safe, way of producing special effects, is to leave them in the hands of a capable trap-drummer who has provided himself with all the hundred and one noise-making apparatuses, now on the market, for imitating everything from a baby's cry of "Ma-ma" to a horse-laugh, "Ha-Ha"; whistles; squeals; imitations of the various sounds made by machinery, *i.e.* sawmills, motors (aëroplane, automobile, motor boats, steam engines, motor cycles) ; shots (cannon, rifle, revolver) ; crashes ; breaking glass ; crumbling of walls ; falling timber ; rain ; thunder ; surf ; tramp of marching feet ; knocks ; raps ; burlesque falls where the hero, a Charlie Chaplin or Fatty Arbuckle, comes to earth with the sound of a clap of thunder assisted by a dozen tin wash-boilers, topped off by a Chinese gong.

There has been much discussion as to whether or not such performance comes under the duties of the organist.   The writers do not think so.   No one can play the organ artistically and at the same time work traps.   It is better therefore to let pass unnoticed such effects as cannot be produced easily and legitimately on the organ itself.   Of course, on the new unit orchestra "organs," these traps are actually a part of the instrument, the organist merely pushing a button or tapping a pedal for a certain effect.

The following are some of the legitimate "special effects" :

Rain — light string tone in quick arpeggii or tremolo.

Wind and rain — light string tone in fast chromatic scales in 3ds, 6ths, and 4ths.

Wind and rain and thunder — all the above with heavy pedal tone, holding down two pedal notes at once when rumble of thunder is desired.

Crash of thunder — any heavy chord, played *sfz* in the lower register, full organ and ped., with immediate *diminuendo*.

Whistles — a minor or augmented chord : 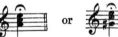 or

Each organist should determine for himself a characteristic chord, by listening to the town fire whistle or to the locomotive, and deciphering the tones for himself.

Bells — Almost every theatrical organ has a set of bells ; hence there is no need of imitation.   On the piano, chimes may be imitated thus :

Glissando — This effect is especially useful in comedy, refined and burlesque.   A slip or fall is emphasized by a *glissando* with one hand followed by a *bump* with full organ, swells closed as desired.   The *glissando* is produced by stiffening the thumb and dragging it up or down the length of the keyboard, using the thumb nail as the point of contact.   The *glissando* is used to illustrate a "slip," sudden descent of an aëroplane, whizzing of an automobile around a corner, any sliding sensation or one of intense speed.

Bump or fall — Slap the keys with the palm of the hand, lower octaves for a heavy fall, upper octaves for lighter effects.

Silence — This is one of the most important and telling effects when properly used. Any extremely tense situation is heightened by a moment's silence, just before the climax is reached.   Suspense, such as when two people, searching for each other, are almost in contact yet each unconscious of the other person's nearness.   In the presence of death, a "close-up" view of a dead person, *absolute silence* is the only adequate description, dramatically, pictorially and musically.

Recitative — Use recitative every now and then to lighten the musical setting, or to heighten a tension.

Xylophone — This stop is useful in comedies.   Use it only as solo, very staccato, with light string acc.

Approaching a climax — Thereby is meant that tense moment when, in a great automobile sweepstakes race, the cars are approaching "death curve," or when we can see them in the distance coming into the final "home-stretch"; or where a man is on a great height and is about to fall, either to safety or destruction, etc., etc.; in such cases a low menacing rumble is of great help in heightening the suspense.   This is produced by a trill in the lower octaves, with soft string and 16' bourdon tones.   Sometimes just a pedal rumble is the thing, produced by holding down two adjacent pedal keys.

Manuals   or   Pedal

(held to-
gether)

This rumble is frequently noticed in the orchestra during acrobatic acts in vaudeville.[1]   When the "thriller" of the act is about to take place, the orchestra stops and the snaredrum begins its subtle, sinister rumble, increasing in volume until the successful fall or jump takes place, when the whole orchestra comes in *fortissimo* to applaud the performance.

Galloping horses — Any music Allegro $\frac{6}{8}$ seems to convey this effect. "Light Cavalry" Overture by Suppé seems to be the most popular selection.

By playing this rhythm softly the effect of distance is lent; increasing the volume of tone brings the horses nearer in the mind of the listener.   A more ambitious player may also study the "Ride of the Valkyries" by Wagner, or "Mazeppa" by Liszt.

Jazz band — The only way to imitate a jazz band is to hear one of these unique organizations.   There is no way of describing it.   Each and every player must hear these peculiar effects for himself and then imitate them according to his impression thereof.   The general idea is to have one hand play the tune, while the other hand "jazzes" or syncopates around it, the pedals performing the drum and double bass parts.   The ability to lift your audience's

---

[1] By careful observance of good vaudeville performances, many ideas may be gained in the way of special effects, particularly for comedy work.

feet off the floor in sympathetic rhythm is the truest test; that you will distress the ears of really musical people goes without saying, but you will not distress their sense of rhythm.   This rhythm on your part must be perfectly maintained, no matter what stunts you may perform with hands and feet.

Feathered animals

Hens cackling —

Rooster crowing —

Birds singing — high flute in trills — chromatically rising and descending

Robins —

Larks —

Cuckoo (or clock) —

(a *minor* third, not major!)

Parrot — Use a light reed tone in recitative in imitation of a person talking.

Grotesque animal sounds

Pigs grunting —

with any tone that will give a ''grunting'' sound.

Donkey braying —

"ROSE OF THE WORLD"

No.	Min.	(T)itle or (D)escription	Tempo	Selections
		REEL No. 1		
1	1½	At screening	2/4 Allegro	Farandole — Bizet
2	1¾	T — Rosamond English	4/4 Moderato	[1] Rose in the Bud — Foster
3	1¼	D — Harry leaves boudoir	2/4 Allegro	[1] Farandole — Bizet
4	1	T — For two months, no word came	4/4 Allegro furioso	Furioso No. 1 — Langey (Battle music)
5	1¼	T — Then the survivors returned	4/4 Tempo di marcia	The Rookies — Drumm
6	1½	D — Rosamond and Berthune	3/4 Andante sostenuto	[1] Romance — Mildenberg (1st part only)
7	3	T — After a time	2/4 Allegretto	Canzonetta — Herbert
		REEL No. 2		
8	3	T — Surely you can help me?	6/8 Poco piu lento	En Mer — Holmes (From Letter D)
9	1¼	T — Before her lay	3/4 Andante sostenuto	[1] Romance — Mildenberg (1st part only)
10	2¼	T — Doctor finds body in queer state	4/8 Lento	Erotik — Grieg
11	1¾	T — So Lady G. sailed for the homeland	6/8 Andantino	Barcarolle — Hoffmann
12	3¼	T — The first day at Saltwoods	3/4 Moderato	Prelude — Damrosch (From Cyrano)
		REEL No. 3		
13	2	T — At last Rosamond sent for Major Berthune	3/4 Andante Cantabile	An Indian Legend — Baron
14	1½	T — It's a letter from Uncle Arthur	2/4 Allegretto	Air de Ballet — Borch
15	1	T — I am secretary of	3/4 Andante sostenuto	[1] Romance — Mildenberg
16	2	T — Then came agony	2/4 Allegro	[1] Farandole — Bizet
17	3	T — A little incident occurred	2/2 Agitato	[1] Implorations Neptune — Massenet
18	1½	T — What an inclosed note told	2/4 Molto allegro	Le Ville — Puccini (Battle music)
		REEL No. 4		
19	2½	T — Prompt, etc.	4/4 Risoluto	Cry of Rachel — Salter
20	2	T — The dregs of life	2/4 Allegretto	Canzonetta — Godard
21	2¼	D — Rosamond leaves table	3/4 Allegro	Appassionato — Berge
22	1	T — Have you noticed any derangement	3/4 Allegretto	Air de Ballet — Herbert
		REEL No. 5		
23	3	T — The breaking point	2/2 Agitato	[1] Implorations Neptune — Massenet
24	3¼	D — Jani enters with urn	6/4 Allegro	Flying Dutchman — Wagner (Overture — omit sailors' song)
25	1½	D — Doctor enters	4/4 Andante moderato	One Who Has Yearned — Tschaikowsky
26	1¼	T — Wounded, Harry escaped	6/8 Allegretto	Love in Arcady — Wood
27	1¼	T — The rainbow's end	4/4 Moderato	[1] Rose in the Bud — Foster

THE END

[1] Repeated Selections

(With kind permission of the "Famous Players-Lasky Corporation.")

CONCLUSION

Having explained in the foregoing what problems the motion-picture organist or pianist has to face, and having shown how to solve them, it behooves the aspirant to such position to provide himself with enough equipment for a trial engagement. Let us now suppose we are setting out for the theater.

Through the courtesy of the film-producing companies, the organist is provided with a "cue-sheet," generally about a week or three days before the picture is shown. Illustration of a sample may be found on the preceding page.

By means of this sheet, the player will select his material, timing the various numbers, the main theme, and the spaces for improvisation. Having selected the music for a picture, place it in proper order within a folder, marked with the name, so that when you arrive at the organ you will not be scrambling here and there and everywhere for scraps of paper.

Tuck your music under your arm and walk into the orchestra pit (where the organ console or piano is placed) with a firm tread and a confident heart. There is no time now for any misgivings. You have entered an electric atmosphere. Whatever you feel personally, you will most certainly convey to the audience. Nervousness, timidity, or fear must be left with your hat in the dressing room outside; they have no place in the auditorium.

Seat yourself leisurely and with confidence. Turn on the lights, arrange your music at a satisfactory angle, and you are ready to begin.

Here we reach an important point. Do not think you have to play frantically *every moment* of the time. This is called most appropriately "crowding the picture." When you wish to change your registration at the end of a theme, take your hands and feet off the keys and change it. *Do not*, above all things, hold a chord church-fashion on one manual while setting up new registration on another. Nor is it obligatory to play during the announcement of "coming events." A little silence now and then is relished by all audiences.

Keep in touch with as many concerns that publish "picture music" as possible.   Renew and enlarge your repertoire as often and as much as you can.   Visit the music shops, whenever you have an opportunity, and look over the novelties in popular music as well as in the better class of publications.   Never lose sight of the fact that you are placed in a position of extraordinary advantage to raise and to improve the musical taste of your audience.   Use wisdom in combining "lighter stuff" and artistic material, work gradually towards a happy union of the two, with music of real worth predominating.

If you are left in doubt concerning any point connected with the question of "how to play for the pictures," the authors will be glad to receive your communication, in care of the publishers, and will endeavor to answer your inquiry as promptly and as satisfactorily as possible.

INDEX

63